MW01055811

A
Pheasant Hunter's
Notebook

By
LARRY BROWN

CAMDEN, MAINE

Cover photograph © 2003 Bill Buckley
(For enlarged prints of this image, contact the photographer at P.O. Box
610, Bozeman, MT 59771, or buck@montana.net)

ISBN 0-89272-608-3
Library of Congress Control Number: 2003105202

Printed at Versa Press Inc., East Peoria, Illinois

2   4   5   3   1

Countrysport Press
P.O. Box 679
Camden, ME 04843

For book orders and catalog information, call 800-685-7962, or visit
www.countrysportpress.com

Dedication

To my late father, Jimmie Brown, who first put a gun in my hands and taught me how to hunt; and to all the companions, human and canine, with whom I've since enjoyed good times afield.

CONTENTS

FOREWORD

I got an e-mail message from Larry Brown this past spring:

"Pretty tough last year—Iowa's all-time low harvest, by a quarter of a million birds. But the dogs gave me some good work, we managed to bag sixty roosters, and the weather was great right up to the end of the season. You should have come out!"

My friend does this to me every year. He knows only too well how much this rooster-hungry Michigan hunter enjoys chasing Hawkeye State ringnecks. I pick my shots for Larry, too, roasting him when he misses out on grouse or woodcock hunting up north with me.

I met Larry Brown in Milwaukee in July 1979, at a meeting of state editors for *Fins and Feathers* magazine. He invited several of us to come to Iowa that fall for pheasant hunting. Larry mesmerized us with glowing talk about sloughs stiff with corn-fed ringnecks—fencerow point after fencerow point; the excellent possibility of shooting a true double. You could hear the passion in Larry's voice and see it on his face and in his animation.

I remember thinking, "This man loves pheasants."

He still does. That's why it is so much fun to hunt with him and why those postseason messages get to me so easily.

For more than twenty years now, I cannot recall a single pheasant hunt in Iowa without the company of Larry Brown. Over such a span of time, men who hunt together can build up quite a portfolio of experience: the Thanksgiving Day thunderstorm that drove us from the field when we realized that our guns were perfect lightning rods; sun-drenched sloughs on one farm; chisel-plowed corn on another, the black clods of earth shining like anthracite; gumbo earth that clung to our boots like black cement on a third.

Sometimes Gene or Steve or Mike or Dave or Chuck hunted with us. Or Larry's friends from college, where he used to teach French: Denny, Todd, Neil. Then there was my son, Brian, who on one November day pricked the carpet-tack spurs of his first ringneck. Three of us shamefully missed that bird before Brian downed it with a 20-gauge single-shot.

The dogs were part of it, too—my Brinka, Macbeth, Chaucer, Holly, Fagin, Sherlock, and Boo; and Larry's own Irish Nick (the Red Rocket); his pointers, Jake and Rebel; his shorthairs, Heidi, Blitz, and Donner; and his Gordon, Gwen. And the others, like Brandy and Briar and Pepper.

Wonderful experiences, all. We slept in motels, motor homes, and farmhouse bedrooms. We ate in truck stops, Amana Colony restaurants, farm kitchens, and a dozen or more no-name cafes and taverns.

Over a period of nearly twenty-five years, you learn a lot about a man who chooses to hunt with you: You learn to take your own birds because he won't contribute to your limit when his is satisfied. You learn to unload your gun promptly at 4:30 each afternoon, the end of legal shooting time in Iowa, even when the pointer has a rooster nailed in the switchgrass. You learn to hunt hard for every lost bird, and then to hunt some more. You learn never to pour motel drinks until the dogs are toweled off and fed, the birds dressed, the guns wiped dry and swabbed.

You also discover that if you are tied up on the phone to

home, Larry will quietly do these chores for you.

You learn not to criticize your partner, even if he takes a bird over your gun barrel. I did that to Larry one fall in Mahaska County. His comment, "I hope I'm being a good host," made me want to sink out of sight in the mud we were slogging through.

You learn not to bad-mouth another man's dogs—even when they bite you, pee on you, and run over your rock-steady pointer. My charges have done all of these things, and more, to Larry.

You learn a lot about pheasant behavior and especially about how, when, and where to best hunt these incredibly cagey birds. Larry Brown is a rooster tactician (maybe it's his extensive military training) with an ever-evolving game plan designed to match their uncanny survival skills. A perpetual student of ringneck ways, Larry writes in his notebook at the end of every hunting day. He jots down things like the weather conditions, how the birds acted, and what went right or wrong with the hunt. He has filled many notebooks since I began hunting with him, but the daily habit goes back far beyond 1979, when we met.

"Why do you take so many notes?" I once asked him.

"Maybe someday I'll write a book about pheasant hunting," he said. "You never know." And write it he did.

This is a new, completely revised and updated edition of that book. I know you will enjoy it.

Tom Huggler
Sunfield, Michigan
August 2002

INTRODUCTION

A dozen years ago, when I wrote the first edition of this book, I thought that I was an experienced pheasant hunter. And, at the time, I'd been keeping notes on every hunt I made for almost twenty years.

This coming season will be the thirtieth during which I've kept notes. After reviewing those three decades of records, I discovered that since the book's first edition the birds have taught me a few more things. So have my dogs and my human hunting companions. Thus, I felt it was time for a revised and updated edition.

It's amazing how those hunting notes refresh my memory of events that have taken place over the course of thirty years. I can have a very clear recollection of an incident, only to discover from my notebooks that I've transposed my human or canine hunting partner or the location in which the incident occurred.

Memory is a tricky thing. For example, here in my home state of Iowa I've talked to hunters my age or slightly younger who claim to remember when a hen pheasant was part of the legal bag. I have to point out to them that hens haven't been legal game since World War II—before they were born, or certainly well before they were hunting. They're probably remembering something an older hunter told them. Where my hunts are concerned, the notes recorded immediately after the events took place keep my memory honest.

I have never claimed to be an expert pheasant hunter. I

think the word "expert" is overused to the point of being almost meaningless. I like the line about an expert being someone with a slide projector and a lecture who's more than fifty miles from home. Today, all too often, an expert is anyone who can post on the Internet.

I do, however, have a considerable amount of pheasant-hunting experience. I'm a native Iowan and have been fortunate to reside in this pheasant-rich state for fifty-two of my fifty-seven years. Although I've spent a good bit more time than most hunters chasing ringnecks, that doesn't make me an expert. I've hunted with people who have more experience than I do, as well as many who have less. And I've learned things from both groups.

My pheasant hunting outside of Iowa is limited to a couple of trips to South Dakota. I do travel to hunt other birds: Upper Michigan, Minnesota, and Wisconsin for grouse and woodcock; South Dakota for prairie chickens and sharp-tailed grouse; Texas and Kansas for bobwhites; and Arizona and New Mexico for desert quail, to name a few of my ventures. But when pheasant season rolls around, I don't often stray beyond the borders of my home state. Iowa, however, has varied topography, and I have shot pheasants from border to border, in well over half of the state's ninety-nine counties. There are significant differences between the terrain and the hunting conditions in western Iowa's Loess Hills, a frozen marsh along the Minnesota border, and a flat cornfield a dozen miles north of Des Moines.

I'd like to have the opportunity to shoot pheasants everywhere from upstate New York to the Pacific Northwest, and all the places in between where they are legal game. But it's tough to drag me out of Iowa when the season's open. Consequently, I'll be telling you about the birds and the habitat with which I'm familiar. However, much of what I have to say will hold true for the pheasant hunting you've done or will do.

I've been writing about pheasant hunting for about twenty-five years. I haven't counted them, but I expect my magazine articles on pheasants number well over a hundred and have appeared in a dozen publications. If you've read one of my magazine pieces, then discover a different viewpoint in this book, don't be surprised. As I said earlier, the birds are constantly teaching me new things. Were that not the case, pheasant hunting might have become boring by now. Instead, I find that I approach a new season at fifty-seven with as much anticipation as I did at seventeen. I hope the birds never cease to interest and challenge me.

I claim no championship titles at trap, skeet, or sporting clays. I was born cross-dominant (right-handed but left-eyed); nevertheless, through practice in the off-season and plenty of opportunities at birds, I've become a better shot than I used to be. But I still miss birds that I shouldn't, and there are undoubtedly many of you who are far more skilled than I am with a scattergun.

My dogs, likewise, are without canine honors. I have owned a variety of them: eleven dogs from six different breeds over the last thirty years. As pheasant dogs, I'd rate all but one as at least average, though most of them were a good bit better than that. While I'd be content to hunt the rest of my days with dogs the caliber of the best ones I've owned, others probably have higher standards. It may be that through experience mine have made up for hereditary deficiencies or training shortcomings on my part. I've also had the chance to hunt over just about all of the more popular breeds that I haven't owned myself, giving me a view of a wide cross section of sporting dogs in pursuit of ringnecks.

This book deals strictly with pheasant hunting and with related topics, such as guns, loads, and dogs. Although the natural history of the pheasant is fascinating, game biologists can do a much better job with that subject than I could hope to do. Likewise, a pheasant dinner can be a true culinary masterpiece. But for pheasant recipes, I'll refer you to any number of wild-game cookbooks written by chefs far more talented than I am.

What you have in front of you is a book about pheasant hunting written by a pheasant hunter. I probably could have summarized this introduction in that single sentence. So with that, I wish you good reading and good hunting.

Larry Brown
Randall, Iowa

ONE

The Evolution of Pheasant Hunting and of a Pheasant Hunter

It is nearly noon on a mid-November day. Nine men are gathered around a couple of cars parked at the end of a cornfield. Shotguns are cradled in the crooks of their arms as they smoke a last cigarette or gulp down the remainder of a thermos of coffee. A pair of teenagers in the group, a bit nervous and slightly apart from the others, check the shells in their pockets for the twentieth time. One breaks open his single-shot 20 gauge and peers down the bore, ensuring that it's not obstructed.

A man of about fifty, wearing a red plaid cap and carrying a 12-gauge pump with most of the bluing worn off, glances at his watch and says, "Almost noon. Time to go. Ed, you take the left. Bill you're on the right side. Boys," he adds, addressing the two youngsters directly, "remember what we've told you. Keep in line. No shots straight ahead once we're past the middle of the field. Uncle Joe and Tom and Charlie don't appreciate getting peppered with pellets." The other hunters laugh at this reference to the three blockers waiting at the far end of the field.

"When you've got a bird down, make sure you get there quick," he continues. "And let's try to shoot all roosters this year," he adds for everyone's benefit. "They're the ones with the pretty feathers and long tails." Everyone laughs.

The group fans out in a line across the eighty-odd rows of standing corn, waiting for the leader to give the signal. He glances at his watch again. "Okay, let's go!" he yells.

The browns and tans of their hunting coats, broken only by the occasional red splotch of a cap, blend in with the yellow of the dried cornstalks and foxtail. The line moves forward at a steady pace down the quarter-mile-long rows. The hunters are spaced about ten rows apart. The object, as they all know, is to herd the pheasants in front of them. They hope the spacing is tight enough to prevent any birds from hunkering down and staying put as the line passes by.

The hunters exchange casual comments as they walk, and pass on an occasional warning to the two novices to stay even with the rest of the line. Some hundred yards into the field, one of the boys spots birds on the ground. "They're running ahead of us!" he yells.

"Just keep going," yells the leader in reply. "Go ahead and shoot one on the ground—if it's a rooster and if it's close enough. But watch your shots!"

At that moment, a rooster explodes two rows to the right and directly behind one of the youths. "Rooster!" he cries. A few seconds of silence, then a gun booms on the far right. "Bill got him," the word comes back down the line. There is a brief pause while Bill jogs into the pasture to the right of the field and claims the first bird of the day.

"Ready down there?" yells the leader. "We're set again," comes the reply down the line. They move on. One of the youths nearly steps on a hen. His gun is up to his shoulder and the hammer back when a yell, "Hen!" from the hunter to his right stops him short.

More shots sound along the line. Two roosters are bagged, and a third hits running. The bird is out of range on the ground and the experienced hunter realizes the futility of chasing the wing-busted cock sprinting down the corn row.

"Cripple running ahead," he calls. "Maybe it'll squat down where we can get it at the end of the field."

The line has now reached the halfway point. "Watch your shots ahead now," calls the leader. The experienced hunters check their safeties in anticipation. They know that the bulk of the action will take place within the next few minutes.

At the far end of the field, three men kneel in a ditch. Spaced about thirty-five yards apart, their job is to stop the birds from running out the far end of the field. All three are experienced hunters, veterans of many drives such as this. They were selected as "blockers" based on this experience, their marksmanship, and in the case of Uncle Joe, his excess weight and his arthritic knees. The men carry 12-gauge repeaters—a Winchester pump, a Remington pump, and Joe's pride and joy, a Browning autoloader with its distinctive, humpbacked silhouette. There are other similarities among the firearms: All have full-choke, thirty-inch barrels, and all serve double duty in the duck marshes.

Joe peeks over the edge of the ditch. The blockers are fortunate to have a position that will keep them out of sight of the pheasants and out of the line of fire of the oncoming hunters. However, they are not overly concerned with the latter. Most of the party are family members, and all are experienced hunters—except the two youngsters, who have been well coached in safety procedures.

"Can't see 'em yet, but I hear 'em coming," says Joe in a loud stage-whisper to the other two, as he slides back down.

They hear a shot from the drivers in front of them. A rooster comes streaking over Tom's head in the middle of the trio. He spins with surprising speed and drops the bird in an open field across the dirt road behind them. The bird hits hard but gets up to run. Tom finishes him on the ground.

"Little behind that one, Tom," chides Joe.

"Son of a gun was really moving," replies Tom with a grin. "From one season to the next, a guy forgets how fast they can fly."

Two birds sail over Charlie's head on the opposite end of the blocking corps from Joe. "Hen! Hen!" he calls twice.

"After last year, I thought you shot them regardless," needles Tom.

"Aw, shut up," Charlie replies. "The sun was in my eyes on that one, but I don't suppose you'll ever forget it."

At that moment a huge rooster, two-foot tailfeathers streaming behind him, explodes from a clump of weeds at the end of the field almost on top of Joe. Tom and Charlie watch with fascination as the old man tracks the escaping rooster. His Browning booms, and the bird drops over forty yards from the gun.

"You're slowing down, Joe," calls Tom.

"Just letting him get out so's I don't shoot him up too bad. Martha gives me a bad time about too many pellets in the birds," he explains.

By now, the line is fifty yards from the fence that marks the end of the field. Birds are flushing in threes and fours. Multiple shots and cries of "Hen!" and "Rooster!" echo up and down the line.

Within fifteen yards of the end of the field, a big rooster erupts directly in front of one of the youths. Gun up and hammer back in a flash, the youngster drops the towering bird in a cloud of feathers.

"Nice shot, boy!" cries Tom from the ditch below as the youngster comes forward to claim his prize. "You nearly dropped that one in my lap!"

The youth beams. The bird is his first pheasant.

The men cross the fence and confer with the blockers on the far side. Tom crosses the road to pick up four birds dropped in the open field beyond. Fifteen roosters met their demise from that single, half-hour operation.

They compare notes. At least three more birds were hit in the air but not dropped, and three or four others were brought down but not recovered. The leader pronounces the operation a success.

"Birds must be down a bit though," comments Joe. "That field's usually good for a couple dozen at least."

Three hunters—the two youngsters and one other—take the birds back to the cars. On the way, as they walk the edge of the field, a tight-sitting bird takes wing right beside them. The veteran drops his load of birds and adds a sixteenth rooster to the total.

A second cornfield yields a dozen more birds The end of the day comes exactly at 2:35 P.M. in forty acres of hay, where the hunters have observed that a number of escaping birds have taken refuge. A rooster sits so tight that the as-yet bird-less youth nearly steps on it. Appropriately, it makes bird number thirty-six, and the twelve hunters have limited out.

Scenes such as the one above were replayed across the Midwest with regularity a few decades ago (they still are in some places, especially South Dakota on commercial hunting preserves). Pheasant hunting has a "group sport" tradition, and opening day was a festive occasion. The block-and-drive method in cornfields was the preferred hunting tactic, especially early in the season.

That tactic worked well in the past for several reasons. Cornfields tended to be relatively small and could be covered by a group of a dozen or fewer hunters. Corn was shorter and easier to shoot over than it is now. Finally, the use of herbicides was less common, leaving more weedy cover in the corn rows to provide hiding places for the birds.

The block-and-drive method was also logical because of the way game departments had set up seasons and shooting hours. In Iowa, for example, the season opened in mid-November and lasted only about a month until 1963, when it was extended through the end of the year. Shooting hours usually started at noon, or certainly no earlier than 9 or 10 A.M. That tradition still holds in South Dakota, where hunting does not start until noon for the first week of the season and 10 A.M. from then on.

There was almost always a fair amount of corn left to be picked by the time the opener rolled around. The late start to shooting hours usually put the birds out feeding in the fields when hunting began. Hence the effectiveness of the cornfield drive on pheasants of forty to fifty years ago.

Gun selection was a direct result of the favored hunting

Thirty years ago, pheasant hunting was more of a group sport than it is today.

tactics. Cornfield shots could be long, which called for a large gauge and a tight choke. Hunters with dogs found that the animals did not adapt well to birds running in standing corn, which meant that canine assistance was relatively rare. To reduce the loss of cripples, hunters opted for the combination that they thought would produce the most kills. A full-choke 12 gauge, the favorite in duck blinds, was also the choice of most Midwestern pheasant hunters.

I remember those days well, though with less nostalgia than do many of my pheasant-hunting contemporaries. They tend to forget the short seasons, the abbreviated hours, and the crippled birds that went unrecovered in the corn.

23

Hunting uncut corn can be productive, though it's difficult for a lone hunter unless he has a reliable, close-working retriever.

Growing Up as Road Hunter

I must admit that at least part of my opinion about the "good old days" can be chalked up to sour grapes. Although I remember seeing those mass drives and hearing about them first hand from my best friend—whose ten- to twelve-man family group always limited on opening day—I seldom participated. I grew up a member of a group that was as welcome by the party hunters as the James Gang at an 1880s bank. My father brought me up in the tradition of the road hunter.

Dad was not only law-abiding, but also highly ethical in all of his other hunting and fishing practices. We didn't exceed our limits while fishing, and we didn't hunt without permission. But there was something about pheasants that brought out my father's outlaw side.

I think it may have been that he first shot pheasants during the Depression, when everyone looked the other way at bending game laws if it meant putting meat on the table. We also lived in what was then just about the best pheasant area of a very good pheasant state. It was hard to visualize the possibility of hurting the bird population.

Not that Dad would exceed his limit, like some greedy hunters who would shoot three birds, drop them off with a farmer, and return to shoot three more. It was his method that was often illegal and almost always unethical.

The party hunters tended to push a good many surviving birds into small pieces of cover adjacent to roadways. The ditches and fencerows along secondary roads could be very productive for those who knew how to road hunt.

With us, it was a family affair. My older brother and I did a bit of it, but I remember it as being more effective when both

Mother and Dad were involved. Dad was the driver and principal shooter. Mother was the scout. I was the backup scout, and as I grew older, I became the backup shooter as well.

Road hunting was simplicity itself. Dad drove the back roads. Mother spotted pheasants in the ditches. Dad stopped and shot them, usually without bothering to get out of the car. If he had to get out—for example, when the bird was on the opposite side of the car—he still shot pheasants on the ground whenever he could. This was illegal in the first case, unethical in the second.

My parents were a great team. from a car moving at thirty-five miles an hour. Mother could spot a rooster with his head a half-inch out of the weeds. Dad always carried his single-shot .410 legally—unloaded and in its case. He was very adept at loading it in the close confines of the car, and he was careful not to cock the hammer until the barrel was out the window.

There may have been another reason my father road hunted. He was a night-shift factory worker who spent most of his adult life making John Deere tractors. He'd come home in the morning, catch a few hours' sleep, then drive out into the country for a quick hunt on the back roads near our home in Waterloo, Iowa. There weren't many people who could have hunted with Dad during the week, and with a very physical job, he wasn't in need of exercise. He just wanted a change of scenery and a chance to put some meat on the table.

For whatever reason, I sensed that this kind of hunting was wrong. It may have been that I read too many outdoor magazines with their discussions of the ethics of fair chase. Maybe I didn't like the ringing sound I'd have in my ears for a half-hour after Dad touched off the .410 inside the car.

Perhaps the thought of going to jail over a pheasant was sufficiently unpleasant. In any case, I was uneasy about the whole procedure.

Although we were definitely breaking the law by shooting from the car, we were no more unethical than many of the party hunters who looked down their noses at those of us who shot most of our birds from the roads. Dad, my brother, and I all shot .410s, yet we probably crippled a smaller percentage of birds than did the big-bore-toting cornfield hunters. We took our shots close and mostly at sitting birds. When we were unsuccessful, it was usually because the rooster ran or flew before we were in position, not because we had hit the bird and lost him.

Some skill was necessary if you were to be a successful road hunter. It wasn't that easy to get within .410 range of a sitting pheasant. If a bird did flush, you had to get that little gun on target quickly if you expected to make a kill. Growing up with a single-shot .410 is undoubtedly why I still tend to rush shots at pheasants.

My own version of road hunting was to get out and walk likely-looking ditches and railroad rights-of-way. After spotting enough pheasants from the car, I got pretty good at figuring out which ditches were the best bets to hold birds. These narrow strips of cover were perfectly suited to a hunter or two working without a dog. We even worked two-man drives, which usually involved me walking and either Dad or my brother driving ahead a few hundred yards, then getting out and blocking for me.

I also developed a couple of helpful tactics when we did spot a bird in the ditch. From experience, I learned that a

27

pheasant would often run or fly if you stopped a car and got out in close proximity. However, if you could make your approach from farther away with some sort of cover, you stood a better chance of getting a shot.

Using the opposite ditch—on the other side of the road from the bird—was one tactic that worked well. If I spotted a pheasant, I'd try to remember its location in relation to a landmark such as a telephone pole, tree, or fence post. Then I'd proceed down the road a hundred yards or so, stop the car, and get into the opposite ditch. I'd stay below the crown of the road, keeping my eyes peeled for the landmark. Once it was in sight, I'd charge across the road hoping to surprise the bird into flushing.

If the opposite ditch wasn't deep enough to provide cover, I'd use the car itself if I had a companion. Once again I'd pass by the bird and continue for at least a hundred yards. Then I'd have the driver turn the car around. I'd walk on the side opposite from the bird, and with the vehicle moving very slowly and giving me cover, I'd work up to my landmark. Once there I'd let the car continue on and charge the spot where I'd last seen the bird. Oddly, moving vehicles seldom spooked pheasants—thus another effective road-hunting tactic.

I offer the above only as historical background, both of pheasant hunting in general and of my own development as a pheasant hunter. I am well aware that road hunting, whether you're inside or outside of the car, is illegal in many states. Although I will still ditch-sneak a bird on occasion, it's mostly for nostalgia. It's certainly not the way I prefer to hunt, nor is it a good example to set for young hunters. It is simply too easy to cross the line into unethical or illegal behavior.

28

Road hunting worked well forty years ago for many of the same reasons that favored the cornfield drive. In those days, Iowa pheasants were mostly concentrated in the northern half of the state, and some of those concentrations resulted in unbelievable numbers of birds. The short season and hours also concentrated hunting pressure, meaning that the birds were being pushed all over. Add to this the pheasant's need to pick gravel in order to digest its food and you had a situation tailor-made for road hunters.

Pheasant Numbers Fluctuate

Times change, and some of those changes are for the better, some are for the worse. The end of the Soil Bank Program in the mid-1960s was not one of the better changes, for either the birds or the hunters. Farming grew more intensive, and with less nesting and winter habitat, bird numbers fell.

That was the pattern from the mid-1960s to the mid-1980s. Pheasant populations shifted to areas that afforded birds the proper mix of food and cover. For the most part, these were places where intensive row-crop farming was impractical. But even the best covers fell far short of producing the concentrations of birds that were relatively common before the end of the Soil Bank.

The 1985 Farm Bill brought about a significant change in the world of the pheasant and the pheasant hunter. Under the provisions of the legislation's Conservation Reserve Program (CRP), some thirty to forty million acres of marginal farmland were taken out of production, much as they were under the earlier Soil Bank Program. The CRP led to an almost immediate and very dramatic upsurge in pheasant populations. For example, Iowa hunters harvested slightly over seven hundred thousand pheasants in 1984—the lowest figure recorded since the Department of Natural Resources has been keeping records. But by 1987, Iowa's harvest had nearly doubled, to almost a million-and-a-half birds.

At peak enrollment, Iowa had just over two million CRP acres. But what Washington gives, Washington can take away. The 1996 Farm Bill reauthorized the CRP, but changed the rules so that some states—Iowa being one of them—lost much of this habitat. Iowa's CRP acreage was cut in half.

The trend under current CRP regulations is away from enrolling large tracts of CRP acreage, other than on extremely marginal and largely unproductive land. Under the 1985 Farm Bill, it was not unusual for entire farms to be enrolled in the program. With the changes of the 1996 law, this practice is much less common.

On more productive land, today's CRP regulations favor practices that target only the most erodible areas. Preventing agricultural runoff and improving water quality are now major goals of the farm program. A "permanent" CRP provision, under which landowners can enroll acreage for up to fifteen years, allows almost anyone with a waterway to establish a "buffer strip" ninety-nine feet wide on either side of the stream. These strips provide long, narrow corridors of habitat, unlike the old blocks of the CRP, which were often one hundred acres or more in size. The current program also emphasizes native-grass plantings over species such as brome. Thus, the tradeoff is smaller areas of better cover for the birds, versus larger areas of lower-quality cover. Initially, wildlife professionals believed that the new program would not be as beneficial to pheasants as the old one. However, having hunted these "habitat corridors" for several years now, I can say that they do indeed provide excellent cover. Pheasants seem to be doing well in areas where buffer strips are common.

New Tactics Evolve

The dramatic drop in bird numbers from the mid-1960s to the mid-1980s resulted in a parallel drop in hunter numbers. Many of those who gave up the sport were the once-a-year gang—the nimrods who went out for easy pickings on opening day. With a resigned sigh and a complaint of "It ain't like it used to be," they returned to the couch and the Saturday football game to which they were better suited in the first place.

While equally unhappy with the decline in bird numbers, dedicated hunters developed new tactics. Widely scattered birds meant that it was necessary to cover more ground in order to find game. Coupling this with the fact that a pheasant in the bag was now a highly prized commodity, more hunters took to using dogs, both to locate scattered birds and to cut down on the loss of cripples. In the Midwest, duck hunters were among the first to make this switch. They discovered that their Labs could be as valuable in the uplands as they were in the marshes.

Such changes did not occur overnight. Unlike grouse, woodcock, and quail, pheasants had never developed a hard-core contingent of devotees. Pheasant hunting had always been an easy game, and its participants were unaccustomed to the adversity that grouse hunters experienced in a down cycle, that woodcock gunners learned when they didn't catch the flights, or that quail shooters knew would follow a harsh winter.

Outdoor writers were also at fault, at least to a degree. Outside of an occasional bit of grudging admiration, mainly as a result of the pheasant's appeal to the masses, where were the hymns of praise to the ringneck? The ruffed grouse had Burton Spiller and William Harnden Foster, the bobwhite quail had Nash Buckingham and Havilah Babcock. The best press the pheasant received in those "good old days" was probably a photo in the *Des Moines Register* of hunters with a pile of opening-day birds. The pheasant just didn't get much respect.

Going to the Dogs

In my own case, it took the odd combination of a classic grouse writer and a Moroccan-born Brittany to show me that it was time to change my approach.

I left the Midwest in the late 1960s and returned in 1973. In between, I read George Bird Evans and shot chukar and European quail in Morocco with a side-by-side shotgun over my first hunting dog. When I returned to Iowa, I brought the dog and the gun with me, along with my new approach to hunting.

For a brief period of time, grouse and woodcock were my first love. Although I now find it hard to believe, my notebooks remind me that there were a couple of years when I actually fired more shells at woodcock than at pheasants. And I did this without leaving the state of Iowa, which even in its worst years is much better ringneck country than it is woodcock territory.

Gradually the truth began to dawn on me. Grouse and woodcock are extremely sporting birds, but mostly so because of where they are found. It's tough to shoot birds you can't see, and dense forest cover sometimes makes it difficult, if not impossible, to even shoulder your gun when birds do make a fleeting appearance.

The pheasant has no such advantages. He lives in places where, in comparison to grouse and woodcock cover, shots are nearly always open. When he flushes close at hand, he is none too fast about getting into the air and relatively easy to hit.

But that isn't the end of the story, as any pheasant hunter knows. The pheasant survives, when he does, because he uses his legs more than his wings. He runs like an Olympic sprinter, and like a world-class boxer in his prime, he just isn't there any more when you're ready to take a crack at him.

Hitting a pheasant is only half the battle. A ringneck is the toughest bird most upland gunners will ever encounter. A couple of No. 8 shot will knock down a grouse, woodcock, or quail, none of which is likely to run far even if still lively when brought down. Conversely, you can't count a pheasant as a sure thing until he's safely tucked into your game pouch, and putting him there can be every bit as much of a challenge as knocking him out of the air in the first place. That kind of tenacity, in my book, is worthy of a healthy dose of respect.

Yet the pheasant continues to get short shrift when compared to "classic" upland birds. Hard-core ringneck chasers who have never seen a grouse or woodcock think that hunting old ruff must be the nearest thing to heaven on earth. I've done plenty of both, and I'm here to tell you that the pheasant should not be shortchanged.

One reason I wanted to write a pheasant book is to emphasize that very point. You can hunt pheasants over solid pointing dogs and shoot them with a classic double, as I do, just as you can grouse, woodcock, and quail. You can also chase them with a champion retriever and a smooth-as-silk pump as do other pheasant hunters. The "classic" aspect of the sport is in your attitude toward the game, not in any inherent advantages or deficiencies on the part of the bird. I firmly believe that pheasant hunting today stacks up favorably with the best upland gunning to be had anywhere in the country. But I doubt that I need to convince many readers of the pheasant's quality as a gamebird.

We pheasant hunters often ignore the fact that it is more a combination of the bird, its habitat, and how it is hunted that makes for great sport than the inherent qualities of the bird itself. Rocky Mountain big-game hunters tree-shoot ruffed grouse for camp meat, and they're often able to get close enough to take the birds with .22-caliber handguns. Grouse aren't hunted there as they are in the East or around the Great Lakes. Even in the Upper Peninsula of Michigan, where I've hunted grouse for several years now, many birds are taken from vehicles on tote roads, much as Dad and I used to take pheasants years ago.

In the Midwest, especially in the prime pheasant states of South Dakota, Nebraska, Kansas, and Iowa, we're now seeing a combination of decent bird numbers and good cover, a mix that results in a kind of pheasant hunting radically different from that of forty years ago. Standing corn is usually hard to find once the season opens, though the birds will still run in it just the way they used to—or even worse because of the lack of weeds between the rows. The really productive hunting takes place in other spots, such as set-aside CRP fields, draws, and waterways.

Because bird concentrations aren't what they used to be, and because additional dog power (as opposed to additional manpower) is required in most cases, smaller hunting parties are much more effective. These days, I wouldn't know what to do with one of those old twelve-man, block-and-drive squads. A brace of good dogs can produce enough birds so that three or four hunters should have a reasonable chance of taking home a couple of roosters apiece.

My appreciation of modern pheasant hunting began when I started using Deke, my Moroccan Brittany, to help me hunt the birds. Although he adapted quickly to woodcock and quail—tight-sitting birds like those he knew in Morocco—Deke never became a first-class pheasant dog. Nonetheless, his occasional points and uncanny retrieving ability made him a valuable companion. I began to prize points on roosters and kills over those points, much as George Evans did in his experiences with West Virginia grouse. I also learned that simply knowing from a dog's actions that there are birds in the vicinity can be a great help to a pheasant hunter. After Deke, I never wanted to be a dogless hunter again.

Deke often operated without a lot of support from his human companion. My shooting was far worse in his first season on pheasants than it is now. Although I was using a 12-gauge double then, I think my pheasant-shooting instincts were still operating as if I were toting my break-open .410. I missed pointed birds that should have been easy. Once, that old single-shot .410 malfunctioned in my brother's hands when Deke had a rooster pinned. Had that dog been human, he probably would have sought out a more capable group of hunters.

Deke made some memorable retrieves his first season. On one occasion, my partner Mark Hanchar dropped two roosters as we worked stripped but still-standing corn in a field where the farmer was finishing his combining. We picked up one bird, but with the combine coming through we had to get out of the way before we could find the second. Although downed birds are notoriously hard to mark in standing corn, Deke found that second rooster on the next pass through the field. In the three short seasons he and I hunted pheasants together, I came to expect Deke to get every bird I dropped. He seldom let me down.

After my Brittany died, my next three seasons were spent trying to convince a mentally challenged Irish setter named Nick that he was really a bird dog. I finally threw in the towel on Nick, after which my luck changed for the better. I saw a pointer named Jake in action at a local kennel and training facility. I liked what I saw, and he went home with me.

Jake could cover a lot of ground in a hurry. I wasn't used to that, but an electronic collar helped me modify his habits and control him without dampening his hunting desire. Jake produced a lot of birds for me, was the classic pointer "statue" when he locked up, and was an atypically strong retriever for that breed.

Unfortunately, most of Jake's hunting career took place in the years before the CRP, when Iowa bird numbers were down and when the cover in the northern part of the state, where I then lived, wasn't suited to a big-running dog. But he showed me what a real pheasant dog could do and set the standards for the ones that have followed.

When Jake died unexpectedly, his daughter Rebel took his place. Rebel had the same bird-finding abilities as her sire, but was easier to handle. She should have had a great career. Pheasant numbers were on the rise, and the thousands of new CRP acres were just right for her. Unfortunately, a kidney disease nearly killed her, then left her capable of only limited duty in the field for the rest of her life.

But I had determined that you shouldn't rely on a single dog if you're a serious hunter, and I'd acquired a young, started (partially trained) German shorthaired pointer when Jake died. Heidi turned out to be one of the proverbial naturals. She didn't need much except exposure to birds—she got plenty of that because of Rebel's health—to complete her training. She hunted the big CRP fields well, and adjusted easier to smaller, thicker cover than did my pointers.

I'd found the style of dog that worked well for me, and I've stuck with it since. As I write this, my canine corps consists of Heidi's grandson, Donner, and great-granddaughter, Dasher. I've also owned one Gordon setter and one English setter in the interim, but shorthairs have been my mainstays. They hunt at a somewhat slower pace than did my pointers, which I appreciate as I near age sixty. And they've all been excellent retrievers, which I consider to be a key quality in a pheasant dog.

As we start the twenty-first century, pheasant hunting has evolved into a challenging game, more closely resembling grouse or quail hunting than it did back in the mid–twentieth century. Although some roosters still fall to dogless hunters, every serious pheasant hunter I know either owns at least one good dog or hunts with a partner who does. Today's gunners operate in much smaller groups, seldom more than four. They treat every rooster in the bag as a trophy and pride themselves on making every possible effort to recover downed birds.

The typical shotgun among the modern, hard-core hunting contingent is different from what their fathers carried. The majority of serious pheasant hunters of my acquaintance carry doubles, either side-by-sides or over-and-unders. Most of these guns have one barrel choked more open than full (often improved cylinder), or if equipped with screw-in chokes they will have an improved cylinder or skeet tube in the first barrel. What these hunters want is a relatively light, fast-handling gun because they know they'll be doing a lot of carrying but not a lot of shooting. As long as it has the capacity to throw at least an ounce of shot out to forty yards with lethal effect, it will do the job. The advance warning a dog gives of the presence of birds makes for closer shots, and of course the dog makes recovering cripples more likely. Nevertheless, most hunters I know would rather bring the bird down close, preferably dead, and not risk the loss of cripples.

I'm much more comfortable with the kind of ethic surrounding today's pheasant hunting than I was with the cornfield gang-hunting or road-scouring tactics of my youth. This is a tradition I'd like to pass on to my son and to the other pheasant hunters of his generation. While not all of the changes have been for the good, I feel that pheasant hunting today is a better sport than it was forty or fifty years ago, and that the majority of today's pheasant hunters are true sportsmen.

TWO

Through the Season

Hunters who think that pheasant season begins on opening day are the same people who are likely to quit the field early, frustrated, and well short of their limits. Pheasant season should start at least a couple of months before the official opener. That's what I feel is the minimum amount of time needed to fine-tune your shooting, spruce up your dog, and find a place to hunt.

I'll talk about guns, shooting, and pheasant dogs elsewhere. I'll also go into detail about how to find places to hunt. For now, suffice it to say that in most states where pheasants are heavily hunted, you need to make arrangements well before opening day if you expect to secure a good place.

In pheasant country, happiness to a ringneck hunter is arriving at his chosen farm on opening morning knowing that he'll be welcome, and that he'll have a reasonable chance of a good day in the field. That "good day" means not only decent shots at birds, but also having enough ground set aside to hunt so that he's not running into other people every fifteen minutes. Even though shotguns are short-range weapons, I get an uneasy feeling when I top a rise and see hunters one

39

hundred yards away and advancing in my direction.

If you have hunting rights to such a spot, count yourself lucky. A friend got me on to a dandy Iowa County farm in the middle of the 1979 season, and I was so impressed with the bird population and the cover that I made arrangements to hunt the opener there the following year. That tradition lasted for seven years and resulted in relatively easy limits on five of those trips. During the other two openers, late harvests and birds taking to huge fields of standing corn made it hard on first-day hunters everywhere in Iowa.

Opening Day

Opening-day birds are usually regarded as easy pickings. This can be true unless, as I mentioned earlier, standing crops cause a problem. But in order to be successful on opening day, hunters have to remember that things have changed significantly since the days of the group hunts that I described in the previous chapter.

The first piece of advice I'll offer is to keep your opening-day party small. If you're trying to get permission to hunt private ground, landowners tend to be more receptive to smaller groups. The only time I've ever hunted the opener with a large group was a year when the Iowa Governor's Pheasant Hunt was scheduled for the first day. That arrangement worked fine because the Pheasants Forever local chapter (Chapter Ten provides a description of this organization) lined up plenty of ground for teams of the sixty-odd hunters involved. With that exception, I've never started the season with more than three other hunters, and many times it's been me and one partner.

Unless you're hunting standing corn, you don't need that

much manpower. There may be a lot of pheasants in a large CRP field, but what you need to find them is four-legged rather than two-legged help. The birds may also be scattered, and even with dogs it may take you some time to cover the ground. But with a small number of hunters, you don't need to find large numbers of roosters to keep everyone interested.

The second thing to remember if you're in heavily hunted country is that you're probably stuck with the farm you start on. Later in the season, if you hunt out one place you can always move to another. On opening day, however, chances are good that you will find other hunters wherever you go in prime pheasant country. That's why many opening-day gunners hunt out their ground, then head for home even if they're well short of their limit and and haven't yet walked themselves into exhaustion. Although this sounds like a disadvantage, you can actually make it work in your favor.

The year 1981 was my first season with my pointer Jake, who was to show me what hunting with a really good pheasant dog was like. It was my second season opener on the Iowa County hot spot I mentioned earlier, and the year before I'd taken a limit without a dog—and missed a lot more birds than I hit.

We started out as a four-man group, but two of them departed birdless at about 10 A.M. That left me and the farmer's son, Todd, with three birds in the bag and everything on the place hunted. We drove to a couple of places belonging to Todd's relatives, but there were hunters everywhere. This didn't surprise me because it was an excellent year for pheasants and we were only about five miles off Interstate 80. There were out-of-state license plates everywhere.

Then I had a brainstorm. It was nearing noon, and both Todd and I were hungry, so I offered to take him to town for lunch. Over sandwiches and french fries, I suggested that we return to his place and start all over again. To tell the truth, I didn't have a lot of confidence in that idea, but I was far from ready to call it a day.

My notebook reminds me that we started our afternoon hunt at about 1 P.M. in the same field where we'd been for the opener that morning. It was an eighty-acre field, about half in picked corn, and the remainder in pasture with a large, weedy draw at the eastern boundary.

Jake found four roosters for us in thirty minutes; two were in a fencerow and two more were in the big draw. One got away by flushing out of range. Two sat tight for points and ended up in our game bags, as did one that didn't wait for Jake to point but didn't flush far enough away to escape the tight barrel of my 16-gauge double.

I theorized at the time that the hunting pressure in the vicinity was pushing birds back and forth all day. The field we hunted that afternoon bordered neighboring farms on two sides, and there were hunting parties both places. They could have chased birds over to us, or they might have chased back birds that we had earlier moved in their direction.

On one other occasion, my longtime partner Mike Carroll and I did the same thing, on the same farm, with similar results. Those two experiences tell me that it is probably a worthwhile tactic if there is enough pressure on surrounding property to chase birds back and forth. In many good pheasant areas, that will often be the case.

Where Are the Birds?

Whether it's opening day or later in the season, where you are most likely to find pheasants depends on several factors.

There are states where it is legal to hunt pheasants a half-hour before sunrise. (I've never hunted any of those states and have often wondered how you tell a rooster from a hen on a dark morning.) Hunting that early, it is quite possible—especially on cold, overcast days—to catch the birds in their roosting cover. Think heavier grass and weeds. If you hunt an area like that later in the day and see depressions and droppings in the grass, file that information away for future reference. You're quite likely to find pheasants there either at the very beginning of legal hours (if you're in an early state) or the very end of the day.

In Iowa, shooting hours have been 8 A.M. to 4:30 P.M. for years. We can occasionally catch birds in roosting cover on a raw, dark day, but more often they're up and moving by the time we can start hunting. While driving, I've spotted plenty of pheasants either scurrying across the roads or flying from roosting cover to food well before sunrise. In a state with a really late start, like South Dakota, save roosting cover for late-afternoon hunts.

When heavy cover is soaked with dew, the birds won't be as likely to spend time hunkered down. Pheasants will hang out in marshes and other wet places, but they don't like to get water on much except their feet. If the cover itself is soaked, they'll look for a place to dry their feathers. You won't see this often during the season, but I've spotted them sitting on fence posts catching the sun to dry out.

As I discussed in the first chapter, pheasant hunters used

to spend quite a bit of time hunting standing corn. I avoid it as often as I can, because without the benefit of one of the block-and-drive attack platoons, working standing corn isn't very productive. And it certainly doesn't promote the best behavior from a pointing dog.

Picked corn is another matter, especially if it features liberal amounts of grass or weeds between the rows. Pheasants are surprisingly good at scrunching down under the stalks. Before the weather turns really nasty, a field like this gives them food and cover in the same place—in other words, just about everything they need.

I used to spend a lot of time hunting Conservation Reserve Program fields. I lived for three years in Poweshiek County, which had about fifty thousand acres enrolled in the CRP. I'd also made friends with Chuck Gates, a lifelong resident of the area. We had permission to hunt several thousand of those acres. With both of us running pointing dogs to sweep the cover, those big grass fields were very productive. In fact, they were so productive that Chuck and I sometimes ignored other kinds of cover.

My notebook reminds me of a hunt we started in typical fashion—walking CRP ground behind a brace of shorthairs. When the dogs didn't turn up anything after the first hour or so, we stopped for a strategy session.

"I can't believe we're not finding anything here," I told Chuck. We were only a couple of weeks into the season, and we knew that bird numbers in the area were very good.

"I can't either," he replied. "Maybe we should try around the corn. They just finished combining a few days ago."

That turned out to be the solution. By the end of the sec-

Early in the season, cut cornfields that are especially weedy can be very good spots to hunt.

ond hour of our hunt, we'd collected two limits. All the birds sat tight for points, and while they weren't right in the picked corn, they were all within gunshot of the field.

This one was easy to analyze once we thought about it. There had been too much standing corn for hunters to tackle during the first several days of the season. When it suddenly disappeared after harvesting, the birds—which had had little or no hunting pressure—felt secure in lurking along the edges, which left them in close proximity to their food source.

Since then, I've found this scenario to be one that often repeats itself. In 2001, because I was out of the country, I missed the opening week of the season for the first time in almost thirty years. When I returned and started checking out

Pheasants will remain in and around harvested corn until harsh weather forces them into heavier cover.

the progress of the harvest on my close-to-home hunting spots, I discovered that one farmer a few miles down the road from me still had quite a bit of corn left to combine. I checked his farm every other day for a week or so. When I saw that he'd finally finished, I knew where I'd be hunting that day.

The key cover feature on his farm is a creek that runs a full mile from north to south. I started at the north end, and I doubt I'd gone two hundred yards before I shot rooster number three. It was the same scenario; the birds were hanging around where their protective cover used to be. But without the corn, they were forced to take refuge in the grass along the creek that cut the field in half. They felt very secure and tried to sit it out, but they were easy targets for my shorthair's sharp nose.

46

As I mentioned earlier, hunting the pheasant opener is almost always good in decent ringneck country unless you have to contend with an excess of standing crops. What happens over the next few weeks will depend on such factors as the bird population, hunting pressure, changes in cover, and weather.

Evaluating Bird Numbers

The game departments of all the major pheasant states come out with population forecasts well before the season opens. In Iowa, local hunters watch for the results of the Department of Natural Resources (DNR) August roadside counts with the same degree of interest that they focus on the prospects for the Iowa Hawkeyes or the Iowa State Cyclones in the upcoming football season. Low numbers and a prediction of a poor season will result in long faces over morning coffee at eating joints across the state.

"I see the birds are down this year," one hunter will say.

"Yup. I sure haven't been seeing many out on the roads," another will reply. "How 'bout you?"

"Nope, me neither. I talked to Ted the other day. He's still got that rural paper route, and he says he can't remember a year when he's seen so few birds."

That was pretty much the consensus in 2001, when the DNR reported the lowest counts on record. However, the counts had been almost as bad in 1993, following historic rainfall and disastrous summer floods. That year, DNR predictions had been wrong. I had my best hunting season ever.

But the situation was very different in 2001. Accurate roadside counts depend on the birds—especially hens and their chicks—coming to the gravel roads early in the morning, where they can be seen and counted. Most years, the chicks are hatched and well grown by August. Although there is little evidence that hen pheasants will produce two broods in a single season, they are known to be persistent re-nesters. If they lose their nest before the chicks hatch—as many of them probably did in 1993 because of the rain and flooding—they will attempt to bring off another brood later in the summer. Most of those 1993 broods were born so late that the DNR personnel probably missed them in their counts. I verified this in my own "survey," conducted with dog and shotgun that season. We were taking a lot of extremely small, young birds for the first month or so after the opener.

But in 1993 the hens also had the benefit of a couple of million acres of CRP in which to nest. About half of that cover was gone by 2001. The birds had also suffered through one of the harshest winters in Iowa history, with many towns and cities recording the most successive days of snow cover ever. Then the pheasants got hit with the double whammy of cold, wet weather during the nesting season.

My own 2001 preseason scouting and training trips with the dogs turned up very few birds. This time, I was fairly certain the DNR's forecast was an accurate one.

The DNR also says that nearly half the annual bird harvest, in a typical year, is taken within the first ten days or so of the season. As I said, I wasn't able to hunt until the weekend after the opener, so I wasn't terribly optimistic when I unloaded Donner, my big shorthair, at a farm not far from home.

The best cover on this one-hundred-and-sixty-acre piece of ground is a creek that flows from north to south. Access is from the north end, and with the breeze coming out of the north that day, my plan was to work the east fencerow south, then hunt back up the creek into the wind.

We weren't one hundred yards from the truck when Donner struck a point. There was more than enough cover on the fencerow to hide a rooster, and this one elected to sit it out. I dumped him on the far side, in the farmer's picked corn.

My side of the fencerow was a bare, harvested soybean field, and when I topped a rise, I spotted a rooster dashing across the open ground and into the cover along a small feeder waterway that dumped into the main creek. We didn't find him, but Donner seemed to be working birds even with the breeze to his back. I decided to continue on south when we reached the main stream.

This creek meanders a lot, which means the cover is quite wide in some places, very narrow in others. Donner got birdy in one of the wide spots, took a couple of steps into the cover, and hit a nice point.

Two roosters broke cover, one headed to my left and the other to my right, but they were about fifty yards out and I resisted the temptation. I walked past the dog a few yards and a third bird flushed, much closer. I hit him hard and watched him tumble into the cover on the far side of the creek.

As I broke my gun to reload, another rooster took wing, angling back toward me and to my right. I closed the gun quickly, swung ahead of the bird, and pulled the rear trigger on my 16 gauge for the easiest shot of the three.

The hardest part of that hunt, which had taken less than a half-hour, was finding the bird that dropped on the far side of the creek. He wasn't dead, but he was hurt badly enough that

This rooster sat tight on the edge of a cornfield—almost tight enough for the dog to catch the bird.

he'd gone just ten yards from where he hit, then buried himself in the heavy grass and weeds. Without the dog, I expect I would have lost him. But Donner had to look only a couple of minutes before his nose led him to the right spot.

Such good luck in what was predicted to be a down year came as a pleasant surprise. Maybe the corn in the neighboring field had been harvested after the opener, and the birds had used it for refuge until then. Certainly the DNR's gloomy forecast had resulted in some reduction of early-season hunting pressure. Whatever the reason, I counted myself lucky to have collected such a quick, easy limit in a season when I figured that we would have to work hard for our birds.

Other entries from my notebooks tell me the same thing: that the best hunting is not automatically over after opening weekend. In 1983, I took a three-bird limit in under thirty minutes on the first Friday of the season. Jake and I were working a small public hunting area—the cover was along a major highway—that had undoubtedly received a lot of pressure the previous weekend.

Two years before that, the same area had given me a brace of birds in well under an hour at a similar point in the season. I could have had number three, which flushed while I was reloading, if I hadn't used both barrels to get number two.

In Iowa, hunting pressure drops off after the first weekend, but most of the nonresidents stay for several days beyond that. The state's twelve-bird possession limit encourages them not to leave too quickly, thus a high percentage of the out-of-staters who come for the opener are quite likely to be around for most of the next week as well.

The situation is similar in South Dakota, where a nonresident license is valid for two, nonconsecutive, five-day periods. With a three-bird daily bag and a fifteen-bird possession limit, most nonresidents are likely to stay for the full five days.

Hunting Pressure and Cover

The opener and the following week is certainly the period of the most consistent and intense hunting pressure of the entire season. Yet my notebooks show clearly that good hunting almost always holds up for at least two or three weeks after the opener. By then, the pressure has dropped off, especially during the week. Nonresidents will continue to visit the best pheasant states throughout the season, but not nearly in the numbers of the opening week.

Although we think of pheasants as fairly smart birds, it

takes them time to adapt to two-legged predators. We some-times forget that the great majority of the roosters we shoot in any given season are only a few months old and have no pre-vious experience evading hunters. Thus, they're likely to be naive about staying out of shotgun range until they've been chased around a bit.

Again, the overall population may be a factor as well. If most hunters get birds quickly and easily, the ringnecks that hang tight in the more out-of-the-way spots may not see humans all that often. Therefore, when hunters do start reach-ing those less accessible corners, the hunting may seem to be every bit as good as it was on the opener.

When hunting is poor on the opener and it's not due to a late harvest, that's an indicator that the season won't be a very good one.

My notes from 2001 describe a birdless hunt in Tama County, just ten days into the season. I'd hunted the same area at about the same time the previous year and found plenty of birds. But in 2001 we found almost none, not even hens. Based on what I saw, I'm pretty sure that even the opening-day hunters in that area went home frustrated.

However, at least in the better pheasant states, bird num-bers are seldom poor everywhere. As I said, heavy rains at the wrong time can mean that few, if any, chicks will hatch. But heavy rains are usually localized. A three-inch rainfall may be recorded in one location, while a few miles down the road, a rain gauge shows only a half-inch.

The moral of the story is that when you find yourself in one of those "black holes" with few birds, try another spot—you may not have to go all that far away. There were some very good areas in Iowa in 2001, and I was fortunate enough to find a couple of them, where I concentrated most of my efforts throughout the entire season. But in general, that was a year when there were far more poor covers than good ones.

Changes in Cover

Throughout most of its range, the pheasant is closely associated with agriculture. In Iowa, farms undergo a drastic change from the beginning of October to the end of November. Standing corn becomes picked corn, and in most cases picked corn becomes a plowed field. Soybeans are the other major crop in Iowa, and a bean field is nothing but bare ground as soon as it is harvested.

Even if most of the crops are harvested by opening day, there will still be significant changes in the cover over the next month. Picked corn, as I mentioned, will still provide excellent food and cover. A plowed field offers some waste grain, but almost no cover. And picked corn that has been worked over by cattle or hogs for some time also loses much of its value for pheasants. Even the weedy draws and creek banks will get trampled into next to uselessness if livestock are there long enough.

This change in habitat may force the birds to look elsewhere for heavier cover, or it may force them into cover that is thinner than they normally prefer. In the first instance, they simply leave those places where you may have found them earlier in the season. In the second, because they sense their vulnerability, the birds are almost certain to be nervous and tend to run or flush wild.

The solution is to change your hunting areas as the season

progresses. Look for better cover, and remember that as time passes you are hunting fewer roosters. As cover continues to deteriorate, you may want to concentrate on places with less pressure. In such spots, the changes in the cover are less likely to have a drastic effect on bird behavior.

Public Hunting Areas

One option is to focus more on public hunting areas later in the season. In this instance, you're making a conscious tradeoff—cover for pressure. Public areas almost always have good cover, but they may receive a lot of pressure, which to a degree offsets the advantage of habitat quality.

I've found that the tradeoff is often worth making. In the first place, public areas may not get as much pressure as you think. They get hit hard early in most cases, because nonresidents are either uncomfortable or unsuccessful in gaining access to private ground. Residents, because of local contacts, usually have an easier time getting permission to hunt private land. For this reason, and because they assume (sometimes incorrectly) that public areas are being pounded, local hunters often shy away from state game areas.

The primary exception to this are public areas that lie fairly close to large cities. In-state hunters from big cities often have the same problems as nonresidents in obtaining permission to hunt private ground. They end up focusing on nearby public areas, thereby increasing hunting pressure and competition.

Two means of avoiding other hunters are to use public areas on weekdays rather than weekends, and to hunt them early in the morning. I've found that if I'm the first vehicle in a public area parking lot, hunters who arrive later will be polite about dividing the cover by taking a "I'll go this way, you go that way" approach, which works well on larger pieces of land. If it's a small area and I'm there first, late-arriving hunters will usually go elsewhere.

I'm often guilty of avoiding public areas when I can get access to private ground. Looking over my notes, I am reminded that such avoidance can be a mistake. This is especially true in years when crops are harvested before the opener, and the early hunting is good on private land. Eventually, as available birds are harvested, the survivors respond to cumulative pressure, and as the amount of cover on private ground is reduced, things start to get tough. Throw in foul weather, increasing the birds' requirements for decent cover, and the odds start swinging in favor of public areas. Under such conditions, take a relatively large public area in good pheasant country and not too close to a major city, and I will almost guarantee that you will find birds.

In 1988, I had consistent—though unspectacular—luck on a six hundred-acre public hunting area that was normally a marsh. In that very dry year, however, the place was virtually wall-to-wall pheasant cover. My notes show that I made five trips to the marsh, hunted just under twelve hours, and bagged five birds. I knocked down two others, but lost them due to a combination of extremely dense cover and dry conditions that inhibited good dog work.

I didn't hunt the place for the first two weeks of the season, but after that I hunted it periodically right up to the end. I moved at least one rooster in range on each visit. As I said, unspectacular but consistent results. Late that same season, I made several trips to good farms and didn't even see a rooster.

Hunting pressure on public areas is heaviest early in the season, but later most of the activity will take place on weekends. As I mentioned a moment ago, if you hunt these areas early in the morning on weekdays after the season is a few weeks old, chances are good that you will have reasonable luck and won't encounter many other hunters.

By way of example, a Minnesota friend of mine and his group had excellent success on public areas in northern Iowa during the 2001 season. They were able to hunt during the week and took birds right up to the last day. And this was during a year when Iowa pheasant numbers were, in general, far below average.

The Impact of Weather

Now that you've spent a fair amount of time reading about bird populations, hunting pressure, and cover, you may be wondering when I am going to get around to discussing weather. I have saved it for last because I consider it to be less important than the first three factors. I know that may seem like heresy, but I have my reasons.

The pheasant is an incredibly tough bird. Biologists from the Iowa DNR tell me that they have never documented a single case of a pheasant starving to death. Even in the harshest of Midwestern winters, pheasants have the equipment and the energy to dig through deep snow and find enough to eat. Look closely at a pheasant's beak and legs and you'll understand why the birds won't die of starvation during Iowa winters.

Although pheasants won't starve, a hard winter will have an impact on their numbers. The winter of 2000–2001 in

Public hunting areas offer good habitat and can be productive, especially late in the season.

Iowa is an excellent example. Heavy snow came in early December, and while there weren't any real blizzards, the white stuff just kept piling up. The winter was also colder than normal, and there was no thaw, as there almost always is in January or February. The colder the weather, the more a pheasant has to eat in order to keep warm. That winter, the birds were forced to spend much more time than usual in the open, scratching down through the snow for food. This made them vulnerable to predation. So while the weather itself didn't kill the birds, indirectly it did result in much greater losses than normal.

Severe winter storms will certainly kill pheasants. If the birds fail to reach adequate cover, they may suffocate if they choose to face howling winds that blow snow into their beaks. If they turn tail to the same winds, the snow can blow up under their feathers, melt from their body heat, then refreeze and encase them in ice.

Fortunately, this kind of weather isn't common, even in the Upper Midwest. Iowa had a "killer" storm just after Thanksgiving in 1985, then went through three winters without blizzards. As I said, although the winter of 2000–2001 was long and cold, there weren't any really serious blizzards. And the following winter was one of the mildest on record, with temperatures much warmer than normal and snowfall well below average.

The contrast between those two winters—2001 and 2002—provides an excellent comparison and shows how relatively mild weather can be just as important as the severe weather events, like blizzards or floods, we tend to remember.

Heavy snow hit Iowa on December 10, 2000. I hunted

three times after that—the last time on December 19—and shot just two birds on those post-snow hunts. After that, I hung up the guns for the season. The snow was simply too deep for me and my dogs to navigate. Because the Iowa season always ends on January 10, that meant I'd missed almost an entire month of pheasant hunting.

During the last month of the 2001 season, I hunted fifteen times (including brief outings close to home) and shot twenty-eight birds, which is very consistent late-season action. But because there was almost no snow, I had to adjust my thinking about late-season birds. One December hunt in particular illustrates this clearly.

The temperature was in the thirties and my partner Dana Dinnes and I had to contend with a strong northwest wind. We started at 8 A.M. working some especially heavy cover along a waterway. All the birds that sat tight were hens, except a lone rooster that Dana put in the bag.

After lunch, we hit another waterway that was especially productive for me that season. We found birds, but they were extremely nervous—as they often are late in the year, and more so when wind is whipping across the fields. If they didn't flush wild and well out of range, they were pulling some other crafty pheasant tricks. On a couple of occasions, my veteran shorthair Blitz dropped off the side of the bank while tracking birds. She made some nice points down in the heavy stuff, where it would have been impossible for us to walk because of the slope. But my notebook reminds me that at least a couple of roosters doubled back on her, flushed behind us, and gave us the slip.

This particular farm has almost a mile-and-a-half of waterway. That year, it had newly planted CRP buffer strips. The good, heavy cover was right along the stream, but the lighter stuff—where the new CRP plantings were only a foot or so high—was where most of the birds seemed to be. And their tactic of the day was to keep low in that stuff and run hard to evade the approaching enemy. They were very successful. Dana hadn't had another shot since his bird early that morning, and my gun barrel wasn't even dirty yet.

We finished the final stretch of waterway, birdless, in midafternoon. I suggested to Dana that we might as well walk the road ditches back to the pickup. I kept Blitz on my side, while Dana crossed over and walked the opposite ditch.

We hadn't gone far before he nearly stepped on a rooster. It was one of those cases where surprise can be the bird's best defense, and that one got away safely.

About the time I was figuring I wouldn't get a chance, Blitz slowed to a creep, then froze. She was in the ditch, while I was in a bare soybean field on the opposite side of a barbed-wire fence. I was about to step over the fence to flush the bird when it saved me the trouble. The rooster lifted into the wind, then swung right across my front for an easy shot. Blitz squeezed through the fence to make the retrieve.

Back in the ditch, maybe one hundred feet farther on, she repeated her performance and a second rooster gave me the same shot as the first. I couldn't believe my luck. When Blitz pointed again, I figured I was at least due for a hen flush. But it was a third rooster, again taking the same trajectory and giving me the same easy shot.

After several hours of frustration, I shot a limit in less than five minutes, from a road ditch with relatively light cover—a place I normally wouldn't have bothered hunting late in the season. In fact, during most late seasons that ditch wouldn't have been huntable; it would have been totally snowed in.

But that year, because of the lack of snow, the birds were using atypical late-season cover. And why they chose that ditch and sat so tight, after running like track stars and flushing well beyond gun range from much better cover, is still a mystery to me. But pheasants are full of surprises, which is one reason I never tire of hunting them. About the time you think you have them figured out, they do something totally unexpected. For the most part, that works to their advantage rather than to yours. In this case, I was very pleased with the somewhat strange behavior of those tight-sitting ditch birds.

But in general, my feeling remains that most of the time, in most places, it is not weather that causes birds to change their habits as much as it is response to hunting pressure and to man-made reduction in available cover.

I do, however, believe that there are two weather factors that significantly increase the difficulty of successful pheasant hunting. The first is a strong wind. While a bit of a breeze is a help in moving scent around for the dogs, it can be a liability when it reaches the twenty-five- to thirty-mile-per-hour range. Wind tends to make just about all game species spooky, and when you're bird hunting and relying on a dog's nose it creates an additional problem.

Given strong winds, my advice here is to hunt sheltered areas like deep draws, stream courses, and the lee side of hills and ridges. Other than that, be prepared for less-than-spectacular dog work and for wild flushes from overly nervous birds.

It is always critical to work good cover into the wind, but es-

In winter, hunt the heaviest cover you can find.

pecially so on windy days. Strong winds carry sound a long ways in open country, and pheasants can hear well enough as it is.

The second negative weather factor is rain. Fortunately, unlike wind, in most places heavy rains are relatively uncommon during pheasant season. When they do come, I have one piece of advice—stay home. If you have limited time, such as on an out-of-state expedition, you may not feel justified in sitting out a storm. Otherwise, forget it.

I've actually seen a number of birds run out from under solid points when it's raining. In fact, the major problem of hunting in the rain—other than keeping dry and warm—is getting the birds to fly. On one occasion, when a bird had the effrontery to squeeze under a fence and go trotting across an open field while my pointer Jake stood there frustrated, I blasted the soaked critter. I don't know if it was a cripple, nor did I particularly care on that day.

In short, my experience is that hunting in the rain produces few good opportunities, but adds significant amounts of frustration and discomfort.

Heat can be a problem for two-legged hunters as well as for their four-legged companions, though its effect on the latter is more severe—dogs work a lot harder than we do. Heat also makes scenting difficult, especially when it's dry. Fortunately, like heavy rains, hot weather—of the seventy-degree-plus variety—is not all that common during pheasant season over most of the bird's range.

Dry weather is another factor that affects dog work. The driest season I can remember was 1988. Clouds of dust rose from the ground with every footfall one made in picked corn. That year, my ratio of lost to recovered birds was the worst it's ever been. On many occasions, with the wind in their favor, my normally reliable dogs would miss birds that should have been easy finds.

Nineteen ninety-nine was another extremely dry fall. My most experienced dog was Blitz, a shorthair with five seasons' worth of experience, who seldom failed to recover crippled birds. She lost more cripples that year than in any other season. And just as in 1988, my dogs had trouble finding birds in the first place.

I did not notice, however, that the drought had much effect—if any—on bird behavior. The main adjustment a hunter has to make in the face of extremely dry conditions is to encourage his dog to work slower and more thoroughly, and to help the dog as much as possible in recovering downed birds. Always carry water in the field, and make sure your dog has plenty of it to drink.

Snow is one weather factor all serious pheasant hunters must face at some point every season, perhaps even for the majority of some seasons. I enjoy hunting in the snow when it first comes. If it stays around too long, gets too deep or too crusty, or is accompanied by extreme cold, it can get to be a real pain.

The first snow of the year seems to confuse pheasants. Considering that the season is often a month old by the time the white stuff blankets the ground, it is surprising that the birds often act as if they've done a memory dump of their experience with hunters up to that point.

In 1995, my notebooks remind me that snow came a bit earlier than normal. The season was only a couple of weeks old when we got a half-foot on the night of November 10. I was guiding then and was supposed to have a party of non-residents coming in, but the snow caused them to cancel. I'd already arranged to hunt a very good farm the next day, so I called in the backup pheasant hunters—my longtime partner Mike Carroll and my son Matt.

That was my ninth season with my shorthair Heidi, and by that time I'd pretty well determined that few birds could out-smart the old gal. The farm we were going to hunt was almost all in the CRP and had excellent bird numbers, but I also knew that it received a fair amount of hunting pressure. My hope was that the veteran dog and the year's first snow would combine to give us a good day afield.

When we arrived at our destination, I didn't have to look too hard to determine that the snow had drifted badly, and had buried much of the CRP grassland. The heaviest cover on the place was along a creek that ran a mile from north to south. Starting on the south end meant we'd be facing a stiff north wind on a day when the chill factor was below zero, but I knew it would help the dog.

After we'd trekked maybe a quarter-mile and hadn't found a bird, I began to wonder whether I'd made a good choice. Matt pointed out to me that he hadn't even seen any tracks.

"I don't think you're going to," I replied. "My guess is they haven't started moving yet. They'll be buried in the heavy cover, underneath the snow. We just haven't found them yet."

He gave me a skeptical glance, clearly not believing in the wisdom of his elders. But just after we crossed a feeder stream and continued up the main creek, Heidi slowed, then locked into a hard point. I told Matt and Mike that they might have to kick around to get the bird up, and one or the other of them must have literally launched that rooster off the toe of a boot. They dropped it on the far side of the creek, but it hit running. I finished it off on the ground, because I knew Heidi would have to struggle through the drifts to get to it.

We picked up a couple more birds before we reached a triangle of heavy cover—mostly horseweeds—bordered by the main creek, another feeder ditch, and a fence. Although we did our best to surround the spot while Heidi crashed around in the weeds, several roosters managed to go out the far side. But we did collect two more there, and another two along the fence bordering a gravel road on the north edge of the farm.

I knew there was heavier cover on the northeast corner, where another waterway below a slight rise provided some shelter from the wind. That would also take us out to the road, which we could follow back to the pickup once we finished our limit—assuming I was right about the birds. And I was.

Matt shot the first rooster over a nice point by Heidi. It was Mike's turn on the last bird. He hit it low and behind, swinging it around. I reached for the back trigger on my 16-gauge double and knocked the bird down with a long shot.

We were done by 10:15 A.M., about two-and-a-quarter hours after we'd started. I conservatively estimated that Heidi had pointed a couple of dozen birds (most of them hens), and we'd probably flushed a total of seventy-five.

Yet we hadn't seen a single track. And when we cleaned the birds, they all had empty crops. My guess had been right. They had hunkered down under the cover and sat out the storm, and had not yet come out to feed by the time we finished our hunt. I've seen that same behavior many times right after a snowstorm; now Matt believes me when I tell him that there are birds around even if he doesn't see tracks. It was a good lesson in the Old Man being right—well, at least on that occasion!

Heavy snow that stays around a long time makes bird hunting real work. Plowing through drifts for a couple of hours will tell you whether your legs and lungs are in shape. During the 2000 season, as I mentioned earlier, it got so bad that trying to hunt was no longer worth the effort.

The worst condition is when a thin crust forms. It's heavy enough to support the birds, perhaps even your dog, but not you. You make more noise than you would walking through two feet of cornflakes, and it's considerably harder work. You probably won't get close enough to the birds to shoot, and if

In the right cover, winter hunting can be productive. This hunter and his Labrador retriever had success working the heavy brush behind them.

you do you may well be so out of breath and so surprised that you'll miss.

One thing a lot of snow does is concentrate the birds into a few spots where there is decent cover. This bunching is a good-news, bad-news sort of deal. For one thing, it's hard to fool that many pheasant eyes and ears. Also, every winged and furred predator in the area is going to be working the same cover. Given the latter, it's easy to understand why the birds get jumpy.

When you've got pheasants in bunches, you tend to have serial or mass flushes. One goes, then another, then they all go. You may get off some shots if you're in range when they flush, but you'd better make them count. It's likely to be a long walk to the next bunch of birds.

In 1985, we had deep snow and cold weather almost from Thanksgiving to the end of the season. It was one of those years when I either had to brave the drifts and try to hunt the bunched-up birds, or stay home. I, for one, can't stand that much inactivity unless conditions are completely unbearable.

I had spotted a flock of about twenty-five birds at a place not far from my home where I had permission to hunt without stopping to ask. The first time I saw the birds, I was driving down a gravel road. Crossing a bridge over a fairly substantial creek, I spied them pecking around like a flock of barnyard chickens on a wide, snow-covered sandbar below the bank.

That particular creek had banks that dropped close to twenty feet from the fields on either side. That very depth was undoubtedly one of the attractions of the place, providing excellent refuge from the howling winds. Those banks also dictated my initial strategy.

In cold weather, pheasants, like this hen, will often roost under grass and weeds. Overnight snow can hide all trace of their presence—except their scent to a dog with a good nose.

I wasn't actually hunting that day, but during pheasant season I'm seldom without a gun and a few shells in my vehicle. When I spotted the birds, I had enough sense to drive on rather than slowing or stopping, which probably would have spooked them. I continued down the road, then pulled into a field a couple of hundred yards from the bridge.

My plan was simple. With the birds directly below the high bank on my side of the creek, I could approach them unseen. The fluffy snow would muffle the sound of my movements.

It worked like a charm. Five minutes later, I was standing on top of the bank above twenty-odd unsuspecting pheasants. Then one of them spotted me, and they flushed nearly in unison. Apparently, I was more surprised than the birds that my simple maneuver worked, because I didn't pull a

69

Snow changes everything, burying most of the habitat the birds have been using. This fenceline looks barren, but it may be the best cover in the vicinity.

feather with either barrel. Those birds learned their lesson quickly. I never caught them in that position again for the remainder of the season.

I did, however, discover that they were almost always somewhere along a half-mile or so of that creek. The difficulty was getting at them. Their favorite spot was a little, willow-choked peninsula that jutted into the creek at one of the stream's few wide spots. That bit of knowledge, as it turned out, was of little use to me.

The problem was that none of my options for approaching their favorite hiding place worked very well. I didn't have the favorable angle that I had used when I caught them under the bridge, and whether I walked the bank on their side or on the opposite side, they'd always see me coming.

I tried coming at the spot from out in the middle of an adjacent field at a ninety-degree angle. That might have worked, except Jake was able to navigate the snow better than I was, and I let him get too far ahead of me. But it did result in one late-flushing rooster in the bag, which was encouraging.

The last day I tried the creek bunch, as I'd taken to calling them, I left the dog at home and decided to walk the ice on the stream itself. This was both quieter and easier than bulldozing my way through the deep snow.

As I rounded the bend, which was within gunshot of the willow pocket, my anticipation increased. My thumb settled firmly on the safety, and my trigger finger rested ready alongside the cold-steel loop of the trigger guard. Fifteen yards, ten, five, one foot in the willows—nothing! Nobody home. The quarter-mile walk back to the bridge was a disappointing one.

Just as I was about to scramble up the bank, I noticed a smaller willow pocket not thirty yards away on the other side of the bridge. When it's the last hunt of the season, you don't leave any cover unhunted.

Even though this willow patch was quite near where I'd first seen the birds a couple of weeks earlier, I was skeptical. I had parked my vehicle almost in sight of it. I walked straight at it across the ice, throwing caution to the winter wind.

I had just planted my feet on terra firma when pheasants began erupting out of the willows, going in all directions. One big rooster climbed nearly straight up, and I dropped him hard on the ice. I swung on a second that had cleared the bank and had the north wind in his tailfeathers. It would have been nice to end the year with a double, but my lead must have been at least a bird length short.

If you're willing to brave the elements, pheasants can be hunted in severe weather with some success. My friend Steve Grooms, along with a fellow Minnesotan, arrived in Iowa to hunt with me on the heels of that harsh, 1985 Thanksgiving weekend storm I described earlier. We went out in a minus-fifty windchill, and we did kill birds. It was neither easy nor comfortable, even with heavy clothing. I tend to think the smart ones were my two pointers, Jake and Rebel, who refused to get out of their doghouses. Steve's springer hunted, and his friend's Lab positively frolicked in the snow. I enjoyed the hunt a lot more when, after the storm broke, I was able to take off my ski mask and no longer had to wait fifteen minutes to get the numbness out of my gloved fingers.

Since then, I'd like to think I've grown older and wiser. I've also switched to shorthairs, and at least the ones I've owned have been somewhat more cold-proof than my pointers. I've also owned a Gordon setter that would play in the snow in subzero weather, and loved hunting in the cold.

I'll still try an occasional frigid hunt, especially if the wind isn't too strong, and if nasty weather has kept me and the dogs inside for a few days. But there are times, perhaps coming with the wisdom of middle age, when I'd just as soon not pay the price.

THREE

Thoughts on Guns and Shooting

The pheasant-hunting fraternity is in a perpetual debate over two crucial questions: Which breed of dog is best for ringnecks, and what gun should a pheasant hunter use? If you are seeking a definitive answer to either, I suggest you look elsewhere. Both questions contain a significant number of variables. But I'm not hesitant about giving my opinion; in fact I will construct a hypothetical "ideal" pheasant gun later in this chapter. As for dogs, I'll talk about them in Chapter Five.

There is so much discussion about gun choice because so many different gauges and actions are employed by pheasant hunters. I've taken roosters with every gauge from a .410 to a 12. Although I haven't used a 10 gauge on pheasants, I'm sure that it sees occasional action.

In America, the pheasant has always been a sort of "every-man's" bird. While plenty of ruffed grouse are taken by those patrolling the North Woods logging roads in pickup trucks, there is also a tradition of hunting them with fine dogs and light, fast-handling shotguns. Bobwhites are hunted with similar custom, largely minus the road warriors.

What you have with pheasant hunting is more of a popular sport; popular in the sense of being available to almost anyone. Traditionally, you didn't need a high-class setter or pointer or a fine gun to chase roosters. The fact that most people pursued pheasants toting whatever gun they happened to own, and often without the assistance of a dog, is why pheasant hunting was largely ignored by "real" bird hunters and, for that matter, by outdoor writers for so long.

As recently as forty years ago—or even less—pheasant hunting was still done the way I described in the opening chapter: gangs of hunters working standing corn, dogless for the most part. Guns of choice were, as I mentioned, mostly 12-gauge pumps or autoloaders, often sporting full-choke, thirty-inch barrels.

But a lot of hunters bagged a lot of roosters with whatever happened to be available. As I've told you, my dad used a single-shot .410, minus a front sight, with the forend taped to the barrel. Of course he shot most birds on the sit, but that wasn't unusual either. I started with the same type of weapon.

Not that I'd recommend that gun, or others like it, to pheasant hunters. Indeed, perhaps a good place to begin this discussion is with what we should eliminate when we talk about pheasant guns.

Shotguns to Avoid

I would immediately throw out two actions and one gauge, and put two other gauges into the questionable category.

The actions I write off for the serious pheasant hunter are the single-shot and the bolt action. Although both are inexpensive and lightweight, that's where the pluses end.

74

You need two quick shots with a pheasant. You may hit a flying rooster and fail to bring him down, in which case you should have a second chance to hit him again. Or you may hit him and bring him down running. In that case, especially if you don't have a dog, you should also be prepared to hit him again. Neither the single-shot nor the bolt action gives you that chance.

Many young hunters are started with a single-shot because it's cheap and, because it's a hammer-type gun, you can tell immediately if it is safe. The problem is that the average youngster has one heck of a time getting the hammer back on most of those guns, especially when wearing gloves. If I had to choose a youngster's first shotgun based on cost alone, I'd go with a bolt action and trust the young hunter to keep it in the safe position until ready to fire. Even better, a youth model pump action (or a used pump) is not much more expensive and provides a quick second shot when the hunter becomes sufficiently experienced to get one off.

Both pump-action and bolt-action shotguns have another important feature for young shooters: The action has to be operated manually before a second shell is chambered. If you give a youngster an autoloader or double barrel, there is a good chance that he may forget to put the gun back on safe after he's cranked off a round. Although that situation can be overcome by allowing the novice to load only one shell, the higher cost of most doubles and autoloaders makes them less practical for a beginner's first gun.

The one gauge I eliminate is the .410. I know that plenty of ringnecks have fallen to the little gauge, including quite a few that I've done in myself. Yes, you can take pheasants with

This rooster offered the hunter an excellent shot, but not one for a lighter gauge.

a .410, but unless you are a skilled scattergunner you're also going to have to pass up some very tempting shots, or risk crippling birds. Unfortunately, many fathers place .410s in their sons' hands based on the fact that they don't kick much. I'll risk a bit more kick for a gun that is much more likely to make clean kills.

The two gauges that I consider questionable are the 28 and the 10. The 10 gauge will undoubtedly kill pheasants, but it's so much gun to carry that I can't imagine why anyone who had a choice would want to tote one. Most 28 gauges are sweethearts to handle, and they pack enough punch to drop roosters at moderate ranges. A 28 gauge is certainly a better choice than a .410 for a beginner or for someone who is recoil-shy. But the 28 gauge performs best with 3/4-ounce loads, which is fine for birds up to ruffed grouse size taken at relatively close range, but definitely on the light side for pheasants. Ammunition for a 28 gauge is also expensive and often quite hard to find in anything other than target loads that are inappropriate for pheasants.

Shotguns to Pick From

The preceding process of elimination leaves us with three gauges and three actions: 12, 16, and 20 and pump, autoloader, and double barrel, respectively. As far as I am concerned, any combination of those gauges and actions will give you the makings of an adequate pheasant gun.

I'm sure pump actions and autoloaders would win a popularity contest today, just as they would have forty years ago. But double barrels—both over-and-unders and side-by-sides—are coming on stronger. There are more of both to choose from now than there were back in the 1950s and 1960s, and they do present some advantages over the magazine-fed repeaters.

Both pumps and autoloaders offer a third shot (or more), and in general (especially in the case of pumps) cost less than doubles. But both over-and-unders and side-by-sides, while limited to two shots, usually have a reliability edge. A jammed autoloader or a short-shucked pump is a more common event than a double that fails to fire its second shot.

Most double-barreled shotguns are lighter and shorter than comparable pumps or autoloaders, making them easier to carry afield. They also make two different chokes available to the hunter, while a single-barreled gun offers only one (without changing choke tubes).

Many doubles also have a harder-to-define characteristic, often referred to as "feel," which seems to make them easier to carry than any weight advantage would indicate. Of more importance to the hunter, a double that feels right seems to almost point itself. There are hunters who make the same claim for their pumps and autoloaders, and some of them are deadly pheasant gunners. But most often, when someone talks about a gun that just seems to be on target when he mounts it, he is usually referring to a double-barreled model.

Many hunters spend several years shooting pumps or autoloaders before they end up with a double. I never had that experience, probably as a result of too much brainwashing by outdoor writers in my impressionable youth. When it came time to lay aside my little .410, I was drawn immediately to doubles.

Although my particular preference was for a side-by-side, fiscal reality prevailed. Dad found me a used Savage Model 420 over-and-under 20 gauge with double triggers. It set me back sixty-five dollars and came with a pretty nice case.

A couple of years ago, I found one just like it at a gun show. Nostalgia went into overdrive and I took it home with me. But I soon found that my tastes had become much more refined in the intervening thirty years. Compared to the guns I own now, that slab-sided Savage had the feel of a two-by-four. Back in my late teens it had been a much better choice than my .410, but it was not a gun about which anyone would write rave reviews.

Over the decades between that first double and the ones

The author's preference in pheasant guns runs to side-by-sides with twin triggers.

in my gun rack as I write this, I've probably had a couple of hundred different shotguns in my hands. But the gun that set me firmly on my present path was my first side-by-side. It was one of the old Ithaca SKBs, a Model 150 in 12 gauge. I acquired it while working at the United States Embassy in Morocco, a country where the bird hunting was good. I shot the Ithaca double quite a lot at at a skeet range on the nearby naval base, and with it I became at least a competent game shot on the quail and partridge I hunted in Morocco.

I returned to America to complete work on a master of arts degree. Shortly after I graduated, I found a 16-gauge Sauer side-by-side in a local gun shop. I felt it would be an appropriate graduation present. Over the next couple of decades, the Sauer accounted for the majority of everything I shot—grouse, woodcock, bobwhites, and a lot of pheasants. Owning that gun refined my tastes from just any side-by-side to one of "classic" configuration—light, fast handling, with double triggers—and caused me to develop a particular affection for that oddball in-between gauge, the 16.

Since then, I've vacillated a bit. I've tried quite a few 12s and 20s, and I even went back to more American-style guns like my first SKB: guns equipped with single triggers, pistol grips, and beavertail forends. But I always ended up returning to what the British refer to as a "game gun": straight or semi-pistol grip (or perhaps a small pistol grip), splinter forend, double triggers. After many years of shooting far better with a side-by-side than with an over-and-under, I can now shoot one style about as well as the other. But when I do select an over-and-under, it too has to have the game gun characteristics.

The author laid out the specifications for this shotgun—an I. Rizzini 16 gauge—with pheasant hunting in mind.

An "Ideal" Pheasant Gun

A couple of years ago, I had a chance to build a pheasant gun from the bottom up, based on the I. Rizzini over-and-unders imported by New England Arms. Once more, I went back to what had worked for me over the years—straight grip, double triggers, solid rib, in 16 gauge. Other than being just a bit heavier than my lightest side-by-sides, that experiment proved to be fairly successful. And the gun had screw-in chokes, an advantage over my other classic doubles.

If someone asked me, "What would you put into the design of an ideal pheasant gun?" the result would be very close to what I did with that I. Rizzini 16 gauge. My thinking runs along the following lines:

81

Action: Side-by-side or over-and-under, take your pick. Both provide two quick shots, reliably, through two different chokes. Both can be light enough for trudging the miles you may have to go before shooting your last pheasant of the day.

Gauge: I chose 16 because it works well for pheasants and represents some weight saving over a 12. But in designing the gun for the majority of pheasant hunters, I'd make it a 12 gauge.

Barrel length: I made mine twenty-nine inches. I used to be a fan of shorter tubes, but I've found that I shoot pheasants better with longer barrels. Twenty-seven inches would be as short as I'd go, thirty inches as long.

Trigger(s): Double triggers are hard to come by on new, mass-produced shotguns, but there's a reason for a pheasant hunter to seek out such a gun. If you're going to have the availability of two chokes, you should also have the ability to select them instantly. For example, when you get a surprise flush at the limit of range and you're only going to have one legitimate shot, why not make it with your tighter barrel? I don't know of anyone who can react quickly enough to operate a single-trigger selector under these conditions, but I know from experience that I can pick the rear trigger rather than the front without any delay.

Be aware that because most pheasant country is also cold-weather country, the double triggers need to be spaced far enough apart so that you can operate them with a glove that's adequately thick to protect your fingers from the cold. Some double-trigger guns scarcely have room for a bare finger, let alone a gloved one. Fortunately, however, many models do offer plenty of space.

Ejectors or extractors: Most new double barrels come equipped with automatic ejectors that expel empty shell casings. They aren't a requirement for me, because with pheasants—unlike some covey birds where you may regularly get delayed flushes—you usually have enough time to pluck out your shells and reload before another rooster takes wing. And with extractors, you're less likely to leave empties scattered about.

Rib: Solid rather than vent. Most side-by-sides have solid ribs, while most over-and-unders come standard with vent ribs. Vent ribs help dissipate heat when you're doing a lot of shooting, let's say at targets. However, they also pick up crud in the field.

Grip: Straight or semi-pistol. And couple that with a splinter forend on a side-by-side, or a small, field-style forend on an over-and-under. The forend shaves some unnecessary weight, as does the grip. For me, that combination seems to work better in the field.

Additional features: Choke tubes are nice for maximum versatility. And I'd also opt for the European tradition of sling swivels. You're seldom in heavy brush when hunting pheasants, and a sling is handy when you shoot your last rooster a mile or so from the pickup.

Weight: I want a gun to weigh no more than six-and-a-half pounds, and preferably closer to six. Many hunters call anything under seven pounds light, because there are a lot of guns out there that weigh well over that.

That's where I would end my qualifications. Not long after I designed the I. Rizzini, I also added a new side-by-side pheasant gun to my inventory. It's a Merkel Model 1620, a 16 gauge built on a 20-gauge frame, and even with twenty-eight-inch

The gun pictured here is a Merkel 1620, a 16 gauge on a 20-gauge frame. Weighing just six pounds but capable of handling at least 1 1/8-ounce loads, it's a gun you can carry all day and still be ready to take a rooster five minutes before the end of shooting.

barrels it weighs just six pounds. It lacks the choke tubes and sling swivels, but otherwise fits my criteria right down the line.

Many shooters who are used to a pump or autoloader do better with an over-and-under, which is similar to a repeater in that it only has a single sighting plane, even though it has two barrels. Some people have trouble adjusting to the broad profile of a side-by-side when they throw it up. For me, this configuration worked fine from the start, but others will have more difficulty adjusting and may not be able to adjust at all.

Some experts will tell you that over-and-unders work better as target guns because of their more precise, single sight plane. It's certainly true that you rarely see side-by-sides in the hands of serious competition shooters. However, there are other experts who say that the broad outline of a side-by-side is actually a plus in the field, because you don't have the advantage of knowing where the target is coming from, or when it's going to appear.

Side-by-sides and over-and-unders work about the same for me, whether shooting pheasants or informal skeet. And while I might break more targets if I shot a gun designed specifically for that purpose, I don't shoot skeet to compete. I'm trying to improve my field shooting, and I'm better off doing that with the same guns I use when I hunt.

A "Fitting" Shotgun

I don't know many serious sportsmen who would go afield with boots that don't fit. If they did, blisters would soon put them out of commission. But there are plenty of hunters who try to shoot pheasants with a gun that doesn't fit. And while that won't land you on the injured reserve list, it will keep you from hitting as many birds as you should.

Whether you like my design of an ideal pheasant gun or whether you shoot a pump action or autoloader, the gun needs to fit you as comfortably as your boots. The concept gun "fit" is well known and understood in Europe, but unfortunately remains a foreign idea to many American hunters.

Whenever you hear someone talk about aiming a shotgun—unless that person is referring to deer or turkey hunting—you should be immediately suspicious. A conventional shotgun has no rear sight as such. Your eye fills this function, and you point the gun at flying targets rather than aim it.

There's only one way in which your eye will be properly aligned with the shotgun barrel when you're shooting birds on the wing, and that is if the gun fits. In other words, you bring it to your shoulder and your eye gives you the proper sight picture, all without having to think about it. When you're shooting birds, there are enough other things that can go wrong without having to worry about adjusting your gun.

Three stock measurements will determine whether a gun fits you. The first is *length of pull* (LOP). This is the distance from the trigger (the front trigger on a double-trigger gun) to the middle of the buttplate. If you bring the gun to your shoulder and the thumb of your shooting hand touches your nose or cheek, or nearly so, the LOP is too short for you. If the gun hangs up on your shooting vest or jacket when you mount it, the LOP is too long.

The second measurement is *drop*. This is the distance between a vertical line extended backward from the rib of your shotgun to two points on the stock. The first point is the comb, or the spot on the stock just above and behind the grip.

The second point is the heel, or the top of the buttplate. If you place the gun upside down on a flat surface, you can measure the *drop at comb* (DAC) and *drop at heel* (DAH) with a ruler. When you mount a gun with appropriate drop, you should see the front sight plus most (perhaps all) of the rib. Some guns, especially older American side-by-sides, have so much drop that you won't be able to see the sight or any of the rib. Obviously, your shooting eye can't align with such a gun, thus you won't shoot it very well.

The third measurement is *cast*, which is a slight amount of bend in the stock. This does not exist at all on some shot-guns, including many American-made guns. But on quite a few foreign guns, especially European and English doubles, there will be a bit of cast. The easiest way to spot it is to hold the gun by the barrel(s), upside down. If the stock is slight-ly out of line with the axis of the barrel(s), your gun has cast. If it bends slightly to the right (when you look at the gun from the stock end), that's called cast-off and is designed for right-handed shooters. Cast-on is a slight bend to the left, for left-handed shooters. Depending on several factors, including the contour of your face and the structure of your upper body, cast may or may not help you. The one thing you want to avoid is a gun that's cast the wrong way—that is, for someone who shoots from the opposite shoulder.

The English and Europeans have done gun fittings for years, and those services are now available in this country at various firearm dealerships and from some shooting coaches. However, you can get a good "ballpark" idea of gun fit through a simple exercise. Pick up your favorite gun (or one you're thinking about buying) and mount it as you would when you encounter a flushing rooster, only with both eyes shut. Once the gun is up, open your eyes. Your shooting eye ought to be in perfect alignment with the rib and front sight. Assuming you didn't have the LOP problems I mentioned earlier, it's a fairly close fit.

If you know the measurements I just discussed—LOP, drop, and cast—taken from a gun that fits you and that you shoot well, those measurements will transfer to another gun. But a word of caution here. There will be some slight (occasionally more than slight) deviations, especially of LOP, if you change from one type of gun to another. For example, my ideal measurements are close to 14 1/2 inches LOP, 1 1/2 inches DAC, 2 1/4 inches DAH, just a slight bit of cast-off, if any at all. These approximate the standard measurements that American gunmakers use, which means I can pick up almost any off-the-shelf gun and it should fit reasonably well. But my LOP is taken from the front trigger of a double-trigger side-by-side. If I switch to a single-trigger gun, my LOP will drop to 14 or 14 1/4 inches. And I have one double-trigger over-and-under that fits me just fine with an LOP of 15 1/4 inches, far longer than I've ever been able to use on any side-by-side.

I should add one final note on LOP before we leave the subject of gun fit. A shotgun that has the right LOP for hunting pheasants in shirtsleeve weather in October may not work when you put on heavy clothing to hunt December birds. Changing recoil pads is one solution to this problem. If you have a stock that's too short for warm weather, you can compensate with a slip-on recoil pad, which you then remove when temperatures drop. You can do the same thing with thicker and thinner fitted pads, replacing the former with the

Thoughts on Guns and Shooting

latter when you wear heavy, cold-weather clothing.

But whether you choose to get a gun fitting, take measurements, use my "eyes closed" ballpark approach, or some combination of these methods, make sure you have a gun that fits. And you'll know that it does when the roosters fall from the sky when you pull the trigger.

What Is Good Shooting?

One of the problems with a light gun, such as I prefer and have just described, is that it can cause a pheasant hunter to shoot faster than necessary. That is something I do too often (I still blame that habit on having started my hunting career with a little .410) and observe frequently in other hunters. The old line that you should "make haste slowly" is appropriate when it comes to shooting pheasants. Nevertheless, because pheasant hunters often end up carrying a gun for long distances with relatively few shooting opportunities, I believe a gun that's on the light side is the way to go.

The difficulty with pheasants is their unpredictability. They may come up in your face, lumbering like an overloaded helicopter, or they may boil up at or beyond effective range. It's very possible to miss easy shots at these birds, although afterward you'll ask yourself how you did it.

Just recently, in the 2001 season, Donner locked up in a road ditch. I had all the time in the world when the bird flushed, but managed to dump both barrels without pulling a feather. Then, to add insult to injury, a second rooster flushed before I could reload. That should have been two in the bag rather than a birdless hunter holding an empty gun.

Pheasants have a reputation of being simple to hit, which

would be accurate if they were all like the chance I just described. But many shots at pheasants aren't that easy, and even when they are, things go wrong as they did for me that day last season.

In 1987, I participated in the U.S. Open Pheasant Championship at the Minnesota Horse and Hunt Club. This event involves released birds, which are typically easier targets than wild pheasants. The Open is a team event, with two shooters and a dog per group. Each team is given twelve shells (six per member) and has thirty minutes to find and shoot six birds. My teammates were hunting buddy Dave Prine, a trapshooting champion, and my pointer Rebel, who was very quick on her feet. Of the one hundred and fifty teams entered in the event, thirty-eight managed to bag six birds. Of those thirty-eight, only three teams scored a perfect six-for-six score. Ours was one of them. (I was shooting better that day!) One of the teams used all twelve of their shells to get their six birds, and four others used ten shells. Because preserve birds generally sit tighter and fly slower than wild ones, this says something about how easy pheasants really are—or aren't—to shoot.

The myth of the pheasant hunter who doesn't miss is just that—myth. I've hunted with some of the best around, and they all miss unless they pass up perfectly legitimate chances.

Back in 1979, I invited three writer friends who are also hard-core bird hunters—Steve Grooms, Tom Huggler, and Gene Kroupa—to hunt Iowa pheasants with me. Neil Montz, an old college friend, was serving as our guide in northern Keokuk County. (Neil is now a Methodist minister, and looking back on it, divine help may well have been involved on that hunt.)

We started the second day of our hunt in an evergreen

grove beside Neil's family farm. It was about three weeks into the season and by that time, as Neil assured us, a wily rooster or two nearly always figured out that the proximity of the farm meant safety.

Neil was right. As our line advanced through the grove, a rooster shot out on Steve's end. It's rare when his Ithaca SKB over-and-under goes off and nothing falls. This time there were two reports with nothing to show.

Such an inauspicious beginning did not indicate what was in store for us during the rest of the day. That rooster from the grove was the first of fourteen we shot at, and it was the only one to make good its escape.

Just how well should a pheasant hunter expect to shoot? I've seen the figure of 40 percent offered as a good average, and I'll agree with that if we use the ratio of birds bagged for shells fired. If we use birds bagged out of birds shot at, I think a respectable pheasant hunter should go at least one for two.

In my notebooks I've kept track of kills-per-shells-fired, although with pheasants a strong case can be made for birds bagged out of those shot at being a more appropriate ratio. I can hit a pheasant well with my first shot, and still need a second, or even a third, to bring down an especially tenacious rooster.

If I kill the first rooster I flush with my first barrel, miss the second bird twice, and take the third with two shots, that gives me two birds for five shells, or a 40 percent average. But that average jumps to two birds out of three shot at, or 67 percent. Few pheasant hunters keep track of such averages, although I think they would find the numbers of interest if they did.

Skeet offers all of the shooting angles you'll see in the field, and when shot from the "gun down" position it's very good practice for hunting.

My best season by far, and not at all typical of my career shooting average, was 1983. Due to job commitments and inclement weather at the end of the season, I didn't hunt as much that year as I often do. I bagged twenty-three roosters with thirty-three shells, which is roughly a 70 percent shooting average. My score based on birds killed to birds shot at was twenty-three out of twenty-six. And I hit two of the three birds that I didn't put in the bag. One dropped and was lost, and my partner finished the other. I had only one clean miss all year. I've had days that were considerably worse than that entire season.

Shooting Practice Is Important

If you keep score and you aren't bagging 50 percent of the

birds you shoot at, there is room for improvement. Any of the clay target games will help, although I think skeet and sporting clays—with birds called for from the "gun down" position—are better than trap. Trap is fine for longer shots at going-away birds, and you'll see plenty of those when hunting pheasants. But skeet and sporting clays will give you a look at every angle you'll encouter afield, plus some you won't. If you can shoot sporting clays at a course where they'll allow you to pass on shots you don't expect to take at pheasants—like springing teal, rabbits, and some of the overly long targets—it's even more helpful.

You'll see a lot of crossing targets on the skeet range in particular, which will teach you the importance of lead. This is critical in pheasant hunting because crossing birds present a deceptively large target area if you include the tail. But what a pheasant hunter has to remember is that a rooster is as long from his rear end to the tip of his tail as he is from his rear end to the tip of his beak. And a shot that's centered on the rear end and the tail will not result in a bird in the bag.

With an overall target as large as a pheasant, you want to be more specific than to just "hit the bird" with your shot placement. You need to think high and in front. They'll all die if you shoot them in the head, but unfortunately—especially on shallow, outgoing angles—not much of the head is visible. If you shoot high and toward the front of a rooster you should break a wing if you don't manage to hit the head, and that will at least put the bird on the ground and give your dog a chance to recover it.

If you shoot low and toward the rear, you may blow a lot of feathers off the pheasant's tail end and perhaps break one or both legs, but that will do you no good unless you knock the bird down.

For most hunters, crossing birds are tougher to hit because of the lead factor. When you do hit them, however, they are much easier to kill. The straightaway flushes, which are simpler shots for most people, are much tougher kills. The backbone is between the gunner and the bird's vitals. That's why the "high and in front" advice is so critical. And on crossing birds, it's almost impossible to lead a bird too much. Practice at skeet or crossing sporting clays will teach you this.

If you are bagging between two-out-of-three and three-out-of-four birds shot at, rest assured that you are among the elite of pheasant gunners. That kind of shooting, if you're taking all of your reasonable shots, is about as good as you're going to do year in, year out. Sure, there will be some years when you have a season like I did in 1983 and kill nearly 90 percent of your intended victims. My friend Steve Grooms once dropped forty-odd birds before one got away. But I wouldn't bet much on that kind of success.

The Bird Is Dead but Doesn't Know It

While the title phrase of this section sounds like a lame excuse for what appears to be a miss, it's occasionally true where pheasants are concerned. I'll use a couple of incidents from the 2001 season to illustrate what I mean.

I was hunting near home in late November, and as far as shooting goes, it was one of those "almost, but not quite" days. I was working down a waterway with heavy cover when Donner, my shorthair, decided to investigate the far side of the creek. When he hit a hard point, I slid down the steep bank, located a crossing point where I wouldn't go over my boot tops, and scrambled up the opposite bank.

Donner was right where he had been, but the bird wasn't. The dog relocated three or four times before he finally pinned the rooster. After all that, I wasn't on target with my first barrel but dropped the bird with my second.

That turned out to be the only rooster we found in that half-mile of waterway. At the end of the property, we followed the fenceline across the south boundary, then turned north on the east fenceline. Halfway back, Donner's beeper signaled "point" in the corner of a patch of thick woods. I crashed through the brush, feeling more like I was hunting grouse than pheasants, to find him pointing right into the fencerow. To avoid trying a shot while tangled in the trees, I detoured around him, crossed the fence, and came at dog and bird from the open field.

The maneuver was a success. I hit the rooster as he curled back over the woods. I lost sight of him as he fell, but I heard him tumbling through the branches. It turned out to be a clean kill, but the recovery took several minutes. Donner and I were looking on the ground, without success, when I glanced up and saw the bird hanging by one leg about fifteen feet up in a tree. The tree wasn't big enough to climb, but it was small enough to shake, and the bird finally ended up on the ground—much to Donner's surprise when it nearly hit him.

We continued down the fenceline and hadn't gone one hundred yards before Donner hit another solid point. I was a bit low and behind on this bird, swinging his rear end hard in a puff of feathers, but he recovered and continued flying. My second shot failed to connect.

I watched as he crossed through an opening in the treeline and headed over a bare soybean field toward the waterway Donner and I had just hunted. He disappeared from sight beyond a rise in the field, but I had a good line on him and we set out in pursuit.

As I topped the rise where I'd last seen the bird, at least two hundred yards from where I'd shot him, I spotted Donner nosing a dead rooster on the bare ground. The bird had made it that far, then given up the ghost.

This is not an unusual occurrence with pheasants. The point of the story is to always keep your eye on a bird you've hit, or even one you think you've hit. They'll often fly on for some distance, then drop from the sky. Such a bird will be stone dead when it hits the ground. This behavior is the result of a pellet that either grazes the heart or clips a major blood vessel. The heart continues to pump blood until the bird expires from internal bleeding. Every time I've dressed a bird like that, I've found its chest cavity full of blood.

On occasion, one of these "dead but doesn't know it" birds will fly straight up instead of horizontally. This is called a "tower." I've seen it happen only two or three times in all the years I've hunted roosters, but once you see it, you won't forget it.

I was hunting a good piece of cover last season with my partner Dana Dinnes. Donner made a nice point and Dana hit the bird solidly, but it didn't come down. I was about to help finish it off when it started climbing. That bird went straight up, well over one hundred feet, then folded its wings and came straight down.

One of the few true doubles I've scored on pheasants

involved both birds doing the "dead but doesn't know it" act. One of them was easy to find because I watched it until it fell, then the dog and I walked to it and picked it up. The other had disappeared through some brush, and although I knew I'd hit it, I didn't figure I'd see it again. But Rebel made a nice point, right where the brushy draw I'd been hunting intersected a fenceline, and sure enough, there was rooster number two dead on the ground.

I could have lost both of those birds had I not kept my eye on one and had the dog not located the other. Pheasants can fly off carrying a lot of shot, so never take your eyes off a hit bird, because after traveling a short distance he may collapse in mid-flight.

Shooting Practice on Feathered Targets

Shooting other gamebirds is another excellent way to warm up for roosters. In most places, pheasant season opens later than seasons for species such as ruffed grouse, woodcock, quail, and doves. Of late, my hunting season has started with several days chasing prairie chickens and sharptails in South Dakota, followed by a trip to Michigan for grouse and woodcock. I'd probably be better off if the prairie-bird seasons immediately preceded the pheasant opener, because the shooting is more similar to that offered by ringnecks than is grouse and woodcock hunting.

Preserves can be good preseason tune-ups as well. Usually, however, I'll shoot quail or chukar rather than pheasants. Both birds are more likely to hold for dogs. They're also a good bit cheaper than pheasants, so you end up getting added shooting for your money, even if it isn't at ringnecks. Another way to make yourself a better shot is to hunt with a good dog. We'll go into this subject in detail in Chapter Five, but briefly, dogs help you in several ways. They will let you know that pheasants are around, will either point or flush them, and will find dead birds and cripples that would otherwise go unrecovered. Even though I grew up hunting dogless, nowadays I'd rather leave my gun home than my dogs.

"Always anticipate the flush" is an extremely valuable piece of advice offered by my friend Dave Prine. In other words, hunt in a perpetual state of readiness. One of "Brown's Rules of Pheasant Hunting" says that a rooster is almost certain to flush when you least expect it.

Dogless hunters may actually have a bit of an edge here, assuming they remain alert. Because humans don't have that all-powerful canine nose to tip them off to birds, they are less likely to be caught off-guard. Take it from me, that can happen when you come to rely on a dog to find roosters for you. And sometimes, due to wind direction or to the vagaries of scent, even the best dog will fail to detect a bird. Nevertheless, a decent gun dog will make anyone into a better pheasant hunter and shooter.

FOUR

Chokes and Loads for Pheasants

In Chapter Three, I discussed shotguns appropriate for pheasant hunting and how to use those guns to hit birds. Other than stating my opinion that a pheasant hunter should use nothing smaller than a 20 gauge, I intentionally deferred a detailed discussion of gauge, choke, and shotshell load to this chapter. My reasoning is simple—the three factors have to be considered together. Too often, writers are guilty of giving fragmented advice in this critical area. Is the 12 gauge best for pheasants? Does a modified choke outperform the other choices? Are high-velocity No. 6s the best shotshell load? These questions are frequently answered separately, when in fact they are interrelated.

Gauge and Choke—Fact and Fiction

Let's begin by getting rid of some myths concerning gauge and choke. Gauge doesn't tell you much except the relative size of the hole at the business end of your shotgun. It is a measurement that was arrived at during black-powder days by determining how large of a lead ball would fit into shotgun barrels. If the barrel would accommodate a solid ball weighing one-twelfth of a pound, it was designated a 12 gauge; one-twentieth of a pound, a 20 gauge; and so on. The .410 is only oddball because it is a true caliber, like a rifle or a pistol, rather than a shotgun gauge.

As I said, gauge is immaterial to a certain extent, because it is what comes out of the barrel and how it comes out that is important, not the size of the barrel. You can shoot light, 1-ounce loads in a 12 gauge, just as you can push heavy, 1 1/4-ounce loads out of a 3" 20 gauge. But all in all, because of its larger bore diameter, the 12 gauge has the capacity to put out more shot than the 20 gauge. However, this does not mean that a 12 gauge throws a bigger pattern than a 20 gauge. This is where choke comes in.

Choke was developed by gunsmiths in the late nineteenth century. Both Americans and British take credit for the discovery. Simply put, choke is a small degree of constriction at the end of the bore that causes a shotgun to pattern tighter and more effectively at longer ranges than if there were no constriction.

Prior to the discovery of choke and its effects on shotgun patterns, all shotguns were made without bore constriction, that is, with what is now called true cylinder choke. (This is a misnomer because cylinder choke is the absence of any choke at all.) Adding choke to a barrel increased the effective range of shotguns considerably, which was an important advantage for hunters, especially waterfowl shooters, in the late nineteenth century.

Since its inception, choke has been more or less standardized by shotgun manufacturers. It is determined by two methods. The first measures the amount of constriction at the end of the barrel. The second method, and the one of importance to hunters, is the percentage of shot the gun will place inside a circle thirty inches in diameter at forty yards. Those figures were arrived at in somewhat arbitrary fashion, but they've survived the test of time. Shotgun choke is evaluated the same way now as it was a century ago.

Table 1: Choke as Determined by Pattern Percentage*

Cylinder (constriction .000")	40%
Skeet (.005")	50%
Improved Cylinder (.010")	55%
Modified (.020")	60%
Improved Modified (.030")	65%
Full (.040")	70%

Source: Black's 2002 Wing & Clay. Amount of constriction listed is for 12-gauge shotguns. Smaller-gauge guns require less constriction to produce the same pattern percentages.

It is choke, not gauge, that plays the key role in determining the size of a pattern. If a full-choke 12 gauge puts 70 percent of its pellets into that magic thirty-inch circle at forty yards, its pattern will be no larger than that of a full-choke 20 gauge, which should produce the same percentage of hits.

In theory that's the way things should work. Of course, you have to compare apples to apples. Using standard 2 3/4", high-velocity shells (such as Remington Express, Winchester Super-X, or Federal Classic) and the same shot size, a pattern should be the same from a full-choke 12 gauge as it is from a full-choke 20 gauge. But there will be a difference in pattern density. In the ammunition I've specified, the standard 12-gauge load is 1 1/4 ounces of shot, while the 20 gauge throws only 1 ounce. For example, No. 6 shot has about two hundred and twenty-five pellets to the ounce, which gives the 12 gauge an advantage over the 20 of better than fifty pellets. However, these extra pellets add to the density of the pattern rather than to its size, making it effective at longer ranges.

This is the theoretical relationship between choke and gauge. If you have guns of different gauges but the same choke, you can check it out yourself on a patterning board. If you do, you will learn why I used the word "theory" here. Bob Brister chose the title for his classic book *Shotgunning: The Art and the Science* for a very good reason. There are probably equal amounts of art and science to shotgunning. Therefore what should happen when choke and gauge combinations are worked out mathematically is seldom what does happen when you go to the patterning board.

Patterning Your Shotgun

It has been said that it is as important for a shotgunner to pattern his scattergun as it is for a rifle shooter to sight in. This is somewhat of an overstatement. The rifleman can literally miss the broad side of a barn if he does not sight in, especially with a badly aligned scope. Because the shotgun is a short-range weapon and the margin of error its pattern allows is relatively large, you won't ever be that far off. Still, patterning is an extremely valuable exercise. It will show you whether your gun shoots where you point it, whether it delivers patterns consistent with the choke marked on the barrel, and which shot size and load perform best in your particular gun.

Earlier, I said that gun manufacturers have more or less standardized their definitions of choke. However, one reason that not all barrels or choke tubes marked "Modified" will pattern the same—and patterns may vary considerably—with the same ammunition is that differences exist in the amount of bore constriction shotgun (or choke tube) manufacturers employ.

In *The Shotgun Book*, the late Jack O'Connor listed the actual bore constrictions used for various choke designations by three major American gunmakers: Browning, Remington, and Winchester. In some cases, there was very little difference. For example, Winchester and Remington used constrictions of .005" and .006", respectively, in their 20-gauge, improved-cylinder barrels. But Winchester and Browning 16-gauge modified barrels had constrictions of .016" and .025", respectively. Since .010" is generally regarded as the difference between two different chokes, such as improved cylinder and modified, it's quite probable that one would get a very different pattern from Winchester and Browning 16 gauges choked modified.

Manufacturers of firearms and choke tubes also disagree as to what pattern percentage a given choke should deliver. Some experts believe that skeet and improved cylinder should both be more open than listed in Table 1—more like 45 and 50 percent, respectively, rather than 50 and 55 percent.

For this reason, many choke tubes are marked not only with traditional designations, but with actual constriction measurements. This does not mean that choke tubes marked .005" from two different manufacturers will throw the same percentage pattern. There may be enough difference in choke taper and length that the same constriction will not guarantee similar patterns.

Quirks like those I've just described, as well as differences between the same shotshell load from different manufacturers, are why patterning is so important to the shotgunner.

What you need to look for on the patterning board is a uniform distribution of shot, a pattern without gaping holes or clustering of pellets. You also want to look for consistency with the same load. For this reason, you should pattern a load several times to see if it is giving you consistent performance.

For most pheasant hunters, a forty-yard shot is a long one. Chances are that you're taking more of your birds at thirty yards, or even closer. Given that, you should pattern and evaluate your choke at ranges closer than the traditional forty yards, especially if it's more open than full. Cylinder bore should throw a 70 percent pattern at twenty-five yards. Skeet should give you that 70 percent pattern at thirty yards, and a modified choke should produce the same pattern at thirty-five yards.

Pattern efficiency for a given choke tends to drop roughly 10 percent for each five-yard increase in range. Thus, a cylinder bore pattern of 70 percent at 25 yards will drop to 60 percent at thirty yards, 50 percent at thirty-five yards, and finally to 40 percent at forty yards (see Table 1). Note that these are "ballpark" figures, and as I'll discuss shortly, they will vary quite a bit between guns and from loads. This system also does not work quite as well for chokes tighter than modified.

Evaluating Chokes and Loads

You should determine if your gun is really giving you the pattern you desire, whether it is tight, full choke or more open, improved cylinder. In order to do this, you must know not only the percentage of hits different chokes are supposed to deliver but also the number of pellets in your load, so you can accurately compute that percentage. Table 2 gives you those figures for the most popular shot sizes used on pheasants.

Table 2: Number of Pellets in Various Pheasant Loads*

Ounces of Shot		3/4	7/8	1	1 1/8	1 1/4	1 3/8	1 1/2
Shot size	4	101	118	135	152	169	185	202
	5	128	149	170	192	213	234	255
	6	169	197	225	253	281	309	337
	7 1/2	262	306	350	393	437	481	525

Source: Black's 2002 Wing & Clay

Note that these are "average" pellet counts, derived from the generally accepted figures for an ounce of shot of a given size. However, pellet count can vary quite a bit, depending on a number of factors such as pellet size, plating, and hardness. For example, I bought a bag of magnum (hard) No. 6 shot for reloading and discovered that the 1-ounce bar on my reloader dropped only about one hundred and ninety pellets. A friend sent me some Baschieri & Pellagri (B&P) nickel-plated No. 6s, and I ended up with two hundred and forty-five pellets through the same 1-ounce bar. Kent's "Diamond Shot" 1-ounce load of 6s contained about two hundred pellets, and Federal's Premium Hi-Brass (copper plated) about two hundred and ten. The obvious difference here is that my magnum No. 6s, as well as the Kent and Federal pellets, were on the large side, while the B&P 6s were smaller than standard.

In general, standard, nonplated lead shot in higher-quality

loads tend to count out the closest to the average numbers used above. But even there you'll find differences. I took apart high-brass 16-gauge loads (1 1/8 ounces of No. 6 shot) from Winchester, Federal, and Remington, and the pellet count ranged from a low of two hundred and thirty to a high of two hundred and sixty-five. But that is obviously better than the difference between one hundred and ninety and two hundred and forty-five pellets in the 1-ounce loads I described above.

If you're into the nitty-gritty of evaluating loads, open different brands of shells and count their pellets. At the same time, take a look at the roundness of the shot. (Round pellets fly straighter than those that are poorly formed.) You can do a "ballpark" hardness test, especially with No. 6 shot or larger, by squeezing the pellets with a pair of pliers and seeing which brands take the most or least force to crush. You shouldn't notice much difference between good-quality loads, but if you find a load with shot that's on the soft side, avoid it. Soft shot deforms more readily, produces more aberrant "fliers," and doesn't penetrate as well as harder shot.

As I mentioned earlier, you should test-pattern your shotgun. Count the pellet holes in each pattern, divide the appropriate totals in Table 2 into your count, and you will arrive at a percentage figure. This will tell you whether your gun is actually producing modified patterns out of a barrel or choke tube stamped "Modified."

But don't expect your shotgun to be perfect as far as pattern percentage goes and don't be surprised to see some variation—perhaps significant—from load to load. For example, I recently patterned five pheasant loads through a 16-gauge, modified barrel. I performed this test at thirty-five yards, a range at which I expected about 70 percent pattern efficiency. What I got were patterns that averaged from a low of 63 percent to a high of 83 percent.

You can actually make such discrepancies work in your favor, depending on what you want your gun to do. In my case, by selecting the appropriate load based on patterning results, my 16-gauge modified barrel will pattern more like skeet or improved cylinder at thirty-five yards and closer to full choke at longer ranges. Or I can opt for something in the middle, with results similar to a true modified choke.

Another problem with choke designations is that there have been significant advances in shotshell design in recent years. If you hunt with pre–World War II shotguns—there are plenty of doubles, pumps, and autoloaders from that era still in use—you may find that your old blunderbuss marked "Modified" is throwing full-choke patterns with today's ammunition. Modern shells are a lot better than what was available when your gun was made fifty to seventy-five years ago. The main improvement is the plastic wad, which causes most guns to shoot tighter patterns than they did with the felt or fiber wads ammunition manufacturers used before plastic came along.

Before I leave patterning and theory and move on to what works in the field, I must mention the last piece of the puzzle—shot string.

What you see on a patterning board is a two-dimensional representation of a three-dimensional pattern. A pattern spreads out not only over space, but also over time. (In other words, not all of a load's pellets strike the target simultaneously.) This time dimension is referred to as shot string.

One of the main culprits in poor shot string performance is pellet deformation. Deformed pellets are not aerodynamically efficient; therefore, they move slower than pellets that remain round. Deformed pellets also tend to veer off-target.

Hard pellets deform less than soft pellets, and large shot deforms less than small shot. In addition, other factors being equal, the larger the gauge, the less likely the pellets are to contact the barrel wall and become deformed. In the smaller gauges, the shot is confined to a shell with less diameter, which makes the shot column longer to start with, hence the pellets are more susceptible to deformation. The extreme example here is the 3" .410 bore, with a shot column that is long in proportion to its diameter.

What shot string means to the hunter is that the load—especially on long-range crossing shots—may string out sufficiently so that the tail-end pellets fail to reach the target on time. It may not make the difference between a hit and a miss, but it can be the difference between a cripple and a kill.

Although the importance of shot string can be overstated, it is a factor that must be considered when evaluating the efficiency of loads. If you don't believe me, read what Bob Brister has to say about it in *Shotgunning: The Art and the Science*. He had his wife tow targets behind the family station wagon to graphically demonstrate shot string. For that undertaking, Brister deserves a medal for perseverance and his wife one for bravery under fire.

Putting Theory to Work

The British on their driven shoots kill more pheasants than we can imagine. Gunners who have money to spend on driven pheasant shooting can kill more birds in a single day than a hard-core American hunter living in a top pheasant state might kill in a season. For example, I've been on a British driven shoot in Scotland. We were eight "guns" total, and in a day's shooting we bagged just shy of three hundred birds.

European driven shoots were even more common in the late nineteenth and early twentieth centuries than they are today. Then it was not unusual for an English sporting gentleman to kill thousands of pheasants in a single season. The marquis of Ripon, who died in 1923, killed nearly a quarter-million pheasants in his lifetime!

Out of this period of extraordinarily prolific pheasant shoots came the writings of one Major Burrard, who applied cold, hard English logic to the subject of pheasant shooting.

Burrard determined that a pheasant offered a shooter about thirty-five square inches of target, approximately half of which was vital area—those parts of a bird's body where a hit is likely to result in a kill. He autopsied numerous birds and concluded that three hits to this vital area, assuming the pellets used had sufficient penetration, would be reasonably certain to result in a kill. His choice of shot was British No. 6, which is a bit smaller than American No. 6 shot. It equates fairly closely to our No. 7 shot, which had almost disappeared in commercially loaded shotshells, but is now making a bit of a comeback.

Other expert opinions are roughly similar Burrard's. Jack O'Connor suggested a minimum of four to five lethal hits with No. 6s to produce a clean kill. Francis Sell felt that it took six to eight hits to be certain of a dead bird. Most experts also specify a minimum amount of energy per pellet. Bob Bell, in his excellent book, *Hunting the Long-Tailed Bird*, recommends three hits in the vital area, with each hit requiring a minimum of 1 1/4 foot-pounds of energy.

A basic rule of shotgunning is to use the smallest shot size that provides adequate penetration. The rule's rationale is that the smaller the shot, the denser the pattern, and the denser the pattern, the more hits there will be on the target.

Although penetration is difficult to measure accurately, retained energy is not. Theories of retained energy necessary for effective pheasant kills range from Bob Bell's low of 1 1/4 foot-pounds to a high of 1 3/4 foot-pounds. Table 3 compares retained energy of various shot sizes at forty yards.

Table 3: Retained Energy (in Foot-Pounds) of Shot at 40 Yards (Average Velocity Assumed)

Shot Size	Retained Energy (Foot-Pounds)
4	4.3
5	3.2
6	2.3
7 1/2	1.3

Table 3 shows why No. 6 shot is such a popular choice and why it is so often recommended. It has plenty of retained energy at forty yards and contains more pellets in a given load than either No. 5s or 4s. (See Table 2 for number of pellets per load.)

But distance to the target isn't the only factor involved in assessing lethality. The British take some long-range and incredibly high birds on their driven shoots, using pellets smaller than our No. 6s. But those birds are coming at the shooters, with their heads and breasts—those vital areas where clean kills will result—exposed to the shot charge. In contrast, most American hunters walk up their birds. Many of the birds we shoot will present some sort of going-away angle, where much of the shot charge will have to penetrate the bird's thick, bony backside before it reaches anything vital. If you shoot nothing but crossers or incomers no farther out than forty yards, an ounce of No. 7 1/2 shot will work fine. But, if you're using No. 7 1/2s on going-away birds, you should limit your shots to no more than thirty yards. Penetration starts to fail beyond that range.

Now let's apply what we know about patterning to what's required to kill pheasants. The standard thirty-inch patterning circle has an area of about seven hundred square inches. If you divide this by Major Burrard's thirty-five square inches of a pheasant's body area, you see that our target covers an area equal to that of twenty pheasants.

Roger Giblin, a British ballistics expert, suggests that every hunter should strive for a 90 percent probability of a clean kill when he centers a bird in the pattern. Giblin further suggests a minimum of five hits per bird to achieve this probability. Our thirty-inch pattern, with one hundred well-distributed pellet strikes, will give an average of five hits per bird. But we also know that patterns don't have a perfect distribution of pellets. And because of the way we determine averages, half of our birds will have more than five hits, and half will have less—and those hit less than five times may not end up being clean kills. Thus, what we should strive for is not an *average* of five hits, but a *minimum* of five hits.

Giblin's mathematical efforts help us here, too. He has computed that you need a patternwide total of eight hits per bird so that at least 90 percent of them will, in fact, receive a minimum of five hits. Eight hits times twenty pheasants (the equivalent of a thirty-inch patterning circle) equals one hundred and sixty pellet strikes, well distributed, to give an effective pattern at whatever range you're shooting.

This begins to tell us something. As a case in point, a 20 gauge choked full and throwing an ounce of No. 6 shot should be good out to forty yards. It also tells us that anything smaller than a 20 gauge is not a good choice for pheasants, unless you want to restrict yourself to shots under forty yards. For example, a 28 gauge with its standard 3/4-ounce load from a true full choke will put only about one hundred and twenty No. 6 pellets in a thirty-inch circle.

Armed with the knowledge of what it takes to deliver an effective pattern, we can begin to make some logical decisions about the proper combination of gauge, choke, and load. Let me add here that there is no magic range for consistently clean kills. Although I'm convinced that most hunters should limit themselves to shots under forty yards, skilled gunners can go beyond that distance. But ranges past forty-five or fifty yards, require tight chokes and heavy loads from a 12-gauge gun. Also, once you approach fifty-yard ranges, due to energy loss you should be shooting No. 5s rather than 6s. And remember that the lower pellet count of larger shot emphasizes the need for both a tight choke and a heavy load.

Selecting Your Choke

Let's assume that you are buying a new pheasant gun and that you've already selected the make, model, barrel length, and gauge. But you're left with the question of choke.

One easy way to solve the problem is to buy a gun with some type of adjustable choke. Although we tend to think of these devices as relatively new, they have been around for some time. The Poly-Choke, for example, has survived the test of time and is still seen in the field.

There isn't much operational difference between the old Poly-Choke and the newer, screw-in choke tubes. Of course the screw-in varieties are prettier—they don't make your gun look like something Eliot Ness used when he was after Al Capone. They can also be used on double-barreled guns, whereas the Poly-Choke cannot.

But, the Poly-Choke has one advantage over the tubes—it is instantly adjustable. You can change your choke simply by giving the device a twist. Screw-in chokes require that you use a wrench and a new tube to make a switch.

There are definite advantages to having a selection of chokes available. When the birds are sitting tight, you can use a more open choke. On those days when the roosters are wearing their track shoes and flushing far ahead, you can change to a tighter choke.

The problem is that you don't always know in advance how the birds are going to behave. After a couple of wild flushes you may decide it's time to twist the Poly-Choke to full or dig out a wrench and another tube. About the time you do that, Brown's Law of Pheasant Unpredictability says that the odds are in favor of the next rooster coming up in your face.

Along with the basic rule of using the smallest shot that will do the job, there is a secondary rule of using the most open choke that will provide an effective pattern at the range at which you take birds. As I stated earlier, a more open choke throws a bigger pattern; thus, it offers a greater margin for shooting error and reduces the possibility of badly shot-up game.

We've already determined that a full-choke 20 gauge shooting a 1-ounce load of No. 6 shot will produce an effective forty-yard pattern. The 16 gauge's standard 1 1/8-ounce load through a modified or perhaps improved-modified choke should also be effective. And shooting a 1 1/4-ounce load, a 12 gauge with an improved-cylinder choke will certainly do the job.

You can also make a pattern less dense—but not bigger—by going to larger shot. This may be what you want to do, for example, if you inherited Granddad's full-choke, 12-gauge pump gun. Personally, I'd opt for opening the choke to improved cylinder or modified, though others might suggest having the gun fitted for choke tubes. But if you want to keep the piece as is, shooting No. 5 shot rather than 6s will give you a pattern that's a good bit less dense.

Another option is to use Polywad Spred-R loads, or if you reload, to insert Spred-R discs into your 1 1/4-ounce, No. 6 pheasant loads. I've patterned off-the-shelf Spred-R loads as well as reloads, and they'll both open a full choke to about improved cylinder. This gives you not only an effective pattern at forty yards, but also the benefits of a larger spread at closer range.

Table 4, which notes the pellet strikes in a thirty-inch circle at forty yards for various chokes and loads, should help you decide what you need to create an effective combination. Once again, remember that these are averages and that different guns, chokes, and brands of ammunition will produce different patterns. In other words, you should still pattern your gun to be certain that you are on the right track.

Table 4: Hits in 30" Circle (40 Yards) by Load, Choke, Shot Size

Load	Choke*	Shot Size		
		4	5	6
1 1/4 oz	Skeet	85	107	140
	IC	94	118	154
	Modified	102	128	169
	Full	119	149	197
1 1/8 oz	Skeet	76	96	126
	IC	84	106	139
	Modified	91	115	152
	Full	106	134	177
1 oz	Skeet	68	85	113
	IC	75	94	124
	Modified	81	102	135
	Full	94	119	157

Pattern percentages assume skeet at 50%, improved cylinder (IC) at 55%, modified at 60%, full at 70%.

Larger Shot Sizes and Heavier Loads

Table 4 shows one of the problems inherent in larger shot sizes. While No. 4s and 5s provide plenty of penetration beyond forty yards, their patterns are quite thin (fewer pellet strikes) in loads of 1 1/4 ounces or less. Of course, at least with a 12 gauge, you have the option of using heavier loads—up to 1 1/2 ounces, without going to a 3" magnum. And there are situations when larger shot sizes might be necessary. Often this is more the "art" side of shotgunning than it is the "science" side.

Near the end of a season, those young roosters you shot at on opening day have several months of additional maturity

What choke and load you use depend on the range at which you shoot most of your birds, which will in turn depend—at least in part—on whether you hunt over a dog.

and have had considerably more exposure to hunters. The birds are bigger, trickier, and their flushes are likely to be wilder—factors that may call for heavier loads.

As a case in point, my notebooks remind me of a December 2001 hunt when I used a recently acquired Beretta 16-gauge side-by-side with barrels choked full and extra-full. For some reason, that day, I carried high-brass No. 5s in my hunting vest rather than my usual No. 6 loads.

I was working a waterway when my shorthair Donner dropped over the side and hit a point near the edge of the bank. I thought I was going to have a close flush and was telling myself to wait out the shot when a pair of roosters flushed from the far side. Neither bird was very close, but I took a chance on one of the pheasants and tumbled him.

Because of the high banks, Donner didn't see the bird fall. I started down the bank, encouraging him to cross the water-way. About that time, a third rooster flushed, giving me a clear, but long, crossing shot. I connected again, and that gave Donner the necessary encouragement to cross over.

It took me a bit longer to find a place in the waterway that wasn't over my boots, and by the time I scrambled up the far bank, Donner had retrieved the second bird. We headed to where the first rooster had fallen. Donner took a couple of whiffs, dropped down the bank, and started working the water's edge. Maybe one hundred yards farther he pointed, then grabbed the first bird. That had been a going-away shot and not fatal, but the bird hadn't gone far.

We continued along the waterway, but didn't move any more birds until we reached a gravel road at the end of the property. A couple of hens flushed from the road ditch, and Donner swung into a point. I thought he was pointing the hen scent when a rooster flushed ten yards behind him. I dropped that bird as well, piling it up against a barbed-wire fence across the road.

I had knocked down three roosters—all long shots—with three shells. One of the birds was wounded, but it was well hit nevertheless. I don't know if the larger No. 5 shot and the Beretta's tight chokes gave me an advantage over my normal choice of 6s. But I do know that I took those long shots with a bit more confidence.

Heavy loads certainly have a place in a pheasant hunter's arsenal, but their use in long-range shooting depends on the skill of an individual gunner. If you connect consistently on shots beyond forty yards—without crippling more birds than you kill cleanly—then you should consider the 12 gauge with heavy loads of larger shot. Back in my guiding days, when I'd sometimes try to finish off a bird that one of my hunters had only feathered, I used 1 1/2 ounces of No. 5s in the tight barrel of a 12-gauge double. That load could kill a long way out when I was on target. But, because I prefer to use light doubles, such heavy ammunition really rattled my teeth.

If you decide to use heavy loads, I'd recommend that you stick with 2 3/4" shells. The 3" magnum is popular, however, especially with hunters who tote 20 gauges but still want to be able to throw 1 1/4 ounces of shot. The problem is that if you're carrying a 20 gauge because you want a lighter gun, 3" magnum loads will provide you with a jolting reminder that you're shooting heavy ammo. Another problem is that you start losing ballistic efficiency when you use 3" shells in a 20 gauge. Although some people swear by them, my advice is to choose a 12 gauge if you plan to use 1 1/4-ounce (or heavier) loads regularly.

Several years ago, I fooled around with a single-trigger, 20-gauge double, using 1 1/8-ounce, short-magnum loads of No. 7 1/2s through an open right barrel, and the same load in 6s through the left. There were two problems with that setup. First, even with an open choke, the 7 1/2s put a lot of shot in the birds. Second, because the gun had a single trigger, I was stuck with an open choke and small shot if a bird happened to flush at thirty-five to forty yards.

By the time I put together the concept of my Rizzini 16-gauge over-and-under as a made-to-order pheasant gun, my thinking had changed a good bit. That custom gun had screw-in chokes and double triggers. I often used an ounce of No. 7s in the first barrel—with an improved-cylinder choke that patterned about 50 percent—for early-season birds. But in my second barrel (thanks to the double triggers I could touch off a shot instantly in case of a long-range flush), I used an improved-modified choke (a pattern of about 65 percent) and 1 1/8 ounces of No. 6 shot. Sometimes I even went to 1 1/4-ounce buffered magnums.

With a bit of thought based on the charts I've provided, some work at the patterning board, and some "field testing" on ringnecks, you should end up where you want to be with your selection of gauge, choke, and load.

Nontoxic Shot

In an increasing number of areas, pheasant hunters are required to use nontoxic shot. For example, lead isn't allowed—even for upland hunting—on most public land in South Dakota. And in Iowa, pheasant hunters must use nontoxic shot around many state-owned marshes and wetlands.

Steel is the oldest form of nontoxic shot and the one with which most hunters are familiar. Although steel shot will work fine on pheasants, you must keep several things in mind if you use it.

Steel pellets are more consistently round than lead, which is good from a ballistic standpoint. But steel is lighter and much harder than lead. In fact, the pellets are hard enough to damage the barrels of many older shotguns. Before you shoot steel, you should make sure that it's appropriate for use in your gun.

Because steel is lighter than lead, you need to use larger

pellets to achieve energy levels similar to lead shot. This, in turn, requires a tighter pattern, though probably not a tighter choke. Because steel does not deform, in general it patterns much tighter than lead. If your barrel shoots a true improved-cylinder pattern with lead, it's likely to pattern at least modified—if not tighter—with steel.

Steel is the least expensive of the nontoxic shot options and is readily available—no small thing to traveling hunters—especially in 12 gauge and usually in 20 gauge. And steel loads are far more efficient today than when they first appeared on the market.

Other approved nontoxic-shot choices are Bismuth, the tungsten alloys (Federal's Tungsten Polymer and Kent's Tungsten Matrix), and Hevi-Shot. Bismuth and the tungsten alloys are ballistically similar to lead, which means you can use the same shot sizes and chokes that you would for lead. And except for Federal's tungsten-iron load, which has been discontinued, they are safe in any gun that will handle modern lead loads.

Hevi-Shot, the "new kid on the block," is ballistically superior to lead. A smaller Hevi-Shot pellet produces energy equal to a larger lead pellet. Although Hevi-Shot pellets are not perfectly round, early tests of the product showed impressive results.

Nevertheless, the jury is still out on Hevi-Shot. Some reports from the field have indicated that waterfowlers weren't getting performance equal to other nontoxic products. Another problem with Hevi-Shot is that it's hard, like steel, which means that it should not be used in many older guns.

I don't hunt waterfowl and haven't shot enough pheasants

with nontoxic loads to have formed my own conclusions. Based on what I've read and what I've heard from hunters who have used someting other than lead, I'd say steel is fine if your gun will handle it. In general, pheasants are shot at closer ranges and with smaller shot sizes than ducks and geese, which means steel should be less of a handicap on ringnecks. For those with older guns, nontoxic products like Bismuth, Tungsten Matrix, and Tungsten Polymer also have proven track records afield. The big drawback of all of these is cost, but it's something we're likely to have to live with as more places disallow lead shot.

Whether you're shooting lead or nontoxic loads, the real test will come in the field. If what you're using puts birds in the bag, in a condition fit for the table, then you've got a winner.

FIVE

Gun Dogs: The Real Pheasant Hunters

At its most basic level, pheasant hunting has three goals: finding birds, forcing them to flush in range, and putting them in the bag. Achieving those goals is much easier and more enjoyable for hunters who have the services of decent pheasant dogs.

Pheasant Fetchers

The Iowa Department of Natural Resources estimates that dogless hunters are likely to lose as many as three of every ten roosters they drop, whereas those with dogs will lose only one in ten. Being a skeptic when it comes to accepting other people's figures and having the database of my notebooks readily at hand, I decided to do my own survey on birds lost. I was surprised at the results.

From 1981 to 2001, I've owned at least average pheasant dogs at all times. During those twenty-one seasons, almost fifteen hundred roosters were shot over my dogs and just sixty-three birds went unrecovered. That's a loss rate of one bird in twenty-four.

Analyzing my notes further, it becomes apparent that

many of those birds were lost when my dogs were still learn-
ing the game. For example, my shorthair Heidi lost ten birds
her first three seasons, while recovering one hundred and
forty-two. A few years later, she had a season where she made
ninety-two retrieves and lost just one bird, and another where
she recovered a hundred and thirty-seven roosters while
losing only two.

The drought years of 1988 and 1999 also had an impact
on my loss rates because of the very poor scenting conditions.
During Heidi's second season, in 1988, she lost three birds
while retrieving only twenty-three—by far the worst loss rate
of her long career. Her pup Blitz, a six-year-old veteran in the
1999 season, lost four birds while recovering fifty-two. The
previous year, she had seventy-four successful retrieves with
one bird lost.

The point is that while you have to make allowances for a
dog's age and level of experience, as well as for particularly
poor scenting conditions, a good pheasant dog should do better than the DNR's number of one bird lost out of every ten
downed. I've had a couple of dogs that I've considered just
average retrievers, and even they recovered fifteen or sixteen
birds for every one they lost.

Some retrieves are bound to be more difficult than others.
A bird that drops on the other side of any kind of obstacle that
slows or stops a dog's progress—waterway, deep ditch, road,
fence—may give a pheasant with two good legs enough of a
head start that the dog won't catch it.

The lengths to which a crippled pheasant will go to
escape are amazing, as is illustrated particularly well in my
1997 notes.

I was hunting my shorthair Blitz, then a four-year-old, on a piece of Conservation Reserve Program ground that bordered Interstate 80. There was a bank thirty to forty feet high leading up to the highway, a slope steep enough that when the dog and I approached the fence separating us from the road, I could barely see the cars and trucks whizzing by above me.

As luck would have it, Blitz pointed within about ten feet of the fence, and the rooster flushed toward the road. I had a safe shot as long as I took it quickly, but it turned out to be too quickly. I only wing-busted the bird, and I watched helplessly as it scrambled up the bank, then dashed across the road, traffic and all, to escape us.

During the 2001 season, Blitz's pup Donner, who was a slow developer compared to both his mother and his grandmother, Heidi, came into his own as a retriever. This process is fascinating to watch and is very satisfying to a pheasant hunter who hates to lose birds as much as I do.

On a November hunt that year, Donner and I were working CRP buffer strips planted in prairie grass that in places was over my head. I was lucky on the first two birds; both held for points in much shorter cover and came down dead in the open.

As we worked the far side of the waterway back toward the pickup, two or three roosters flushed that I might have shot at if I'd been hunting with a more experienced retriever. But they were long shots over the tall grass, where it's difficult for both man and dog to mark a bird's fall, and I decided to pass.

My chance finally came when Donner slammed on point right at the edge of the tall grass. The bird flushed in front of

Donner, the author's German shorthair, points with authority indicating that "There's a bird right here!"

him, and I dropped it over the high cover. I followed the dog into the grass, figuring he'd find a dead rooster close to the outside edge of the strip. But he came up empty. When we emerged into the harvested corn on the far side, Donner seemed to pick up scent, raced back and forth a couple of times, acting like one of my veteran dogs on a hot trail.

I dropped my orange hat where we were, thinking he might be trailing another bird and that the shot rooster was lying dead in the grass. When birds come down dead and don't move when they hit, they often put out very little scent and can be tough to find. I've seen dogs stand on or right over these birds without realizing they were there.

But Donner seemed sure of what he was doing, so I followed him. About two hundred yards farther down, two

In heavy-grass fields such as this, you'll need a dog to recover birds unless they come down stone dead.

waterways joined. Donner cut through the heavy grass toward the larger waterway and I lost sight of him. Then I heard his beeper go into the "point" mode. I found him locked up, down off the steep bank. Once there, I gave him the "Fetch" command. He dove off the bank and grabbed the bird from beneath a clump of overhanging weeds, where it had sought shelter. That would have been an excellent recovery for a veteran, but I was especially pleased to see such nice work from an inexperienced dog.

During the 2000 season, Donner's mother, Blitz, found one that nearly got away, a bird that showed me, once again, just how tough pheasants can be.

I had already collected two roosters over nice points by Blitz. We were hunting buffer strips thick with willows and other heavy streamside cover, in addition to normal prairie grass. With two birds in the bag, I'd decided to walk the fall-plowed field on the outside edge of the heavy stuff, where the going was easier.

Blitz caught scent, and I heard her bell go silent somewhere in the middle of the head-high grass. I moved in cautiously and spotted her just about the time the rooster decided he'd better leave. The shot wasn't long, but I had to take it quickly because of the tall grass in my face. The bird, which had headed toward the waterway, looked to be hit hard, and Blitz and I had a good line to follow.

It took us thirty seconds, at most, to reach where the bird should have been. Blitz took a couple of sniffs, ran down the bank to the edge of the water, turned around, and repeated her performance. Then she started following the bank in the opposite direction. That led, very shortly, to a point in thick cover. I walked in, expecting her to grab my rooster, but a hen flushed in my face. Then she pointed another hen. I began to think that all the bird scent might be confusing her, and causing her to lose the trail.

We doubled back to where she had first picked up the bird's scent. Once more she went down to the water's edge. But she didn't stop there; instead she swam across the stream and clambered up the far slope. As soon as she hit the top of the bank, she locked on point.

I called "Dead bird—Fetch," hoping she'd found the cripple. She dove into the grass, then came back across the creek with the rooster that was very much alive. With both wings and one leg broken, he'd managed to hobble along the bank for twenty yards, swim the creek (yes, pheasants can swim,

Here's a group of pheasant hunters that's well prepared in terms of dog power.

although they don't like to), and bury himself in the cover on the far side. That would have been an impossible recovery without a dog, and an unlikely one without an experienced and tenacious retriever.

The Myth of Best Breed

Retrieving downed birds is only one of the three goals I mentioned at the start of this chapter. I began with it because it is the easiest to quantify from my notebooks. But I am convinced, as are various game commissions and other organizations with access to data on the subject, that in addition to recovering dead and crippled roosters dogs will also help pheasant hunters find more birds in the first place.

Which breed of dog ranks at the top of the heap for a pheasant hunter? That is a difficult question. There is no one "right" choice of breed that will satisfy all hunters. Indeed, there are as many different opinions on pheasant dogs as there are on the choice of gauge, choke, and shotshell. But unlike guns and loads, with dogs we can't really rely on facts and figures. What we have to go by are personal preferences and gut feelings.

I once gave some thought to devising a scale for evaluating the potential of various breeds as pheasant dogs. I thought about including such factors as range, retrieving ability, trainability, and tolerance for cold weather. I considered using a numerical scale of one to five for each category and adding the total score to come up with the best breed.

Unfortunately this approach didn't work. While one can make some generalizations—such as Labradors are far more cold-tolerant than pointers, and springer spaniels are better natural retrievers than English setters—there are too many differences between individual dogs of any given breed to accurately rate and compare breeds as a whole.

Even the decision of whether to go with a pointing or a flushing breed is a question of individual hunter preference. Both have advantages and disadvantages.

Pheasant hunters should be a skeptical not only of generalizations about breeds of dogs, but also of people I refer to as "breed fanatics." These folks raise one particular breed of dog, and they have a vested interest in convincing potential buyers that their "curly-coated pointing bloodhounds" are the finest pheasant dogs ever developed.

In terms of selecting a gun dog, the best advice I can offer is to do business with a kennel that has a reputation for producing good hunters. If you have a hunting companion whose dog you admire, find out where he got it. The chances are relatively high that a dog from the same bloodlines will also be a good hunter. Keep in mind that there may be nearly as much difference between bloodlines within breeds as there is between one breed and another. The problem is that the difference may not be apparent until you see dogs from different lines in the field. And be particularly cautious with those breeds that have distinct show and hunting bloodlines.

Top shooting preserves can be good places to go if you are looking for a hunting dog. Some of them produce their own stock, and they often have more than one breed available. Chances are high, because of the nature of their business, that they will not be breeding show dogs.

There is no single breed of gun dog as closely identified with pheasant hunting as the pointer is with bobwhite quail, or the English setter with ruffed grouse. This may be due to the fact that pheasants are hunted in such a wide variety of cover, or that pheasants are thought of as more "blue collar" birds than are either quail or grouse. The devotees of the latter two birds have elevated their pursuit to an almost ethereal level. Pheasant hunting, on the other hand, has always had more to do with putting meat on the table than with sporting tradition. Just as pheasant hunters have often grabbed whatever gun was handy, they have also used whatever breed of dog they happened to own. Thus, a pointer acquired to hunt quail or a Labrador retriever purchased for waterfowling could both end up doing double duty on pheasants

I do want to put one long-standing myth to rest. Pointing dogs can handle pheasants and, in fact, can do so very well. My first really good pheasant dog, Jake, was a pointer—a

If this bird's a rooster, it's in trouble, trapped as it is between Heidi and approaching hunters.

breed not overly popular among pheasant hunters, nor noted for producing especially skilled retrievers. Jake was very good at both finding birds in the first place and bringing running cripples to bag.

The Iron Lady

For me, however, the standard was set by my first German shorthaired pointer. Heidi had some definite advantages. Her first season was 1987, when the CRP really took hold in Iowa and our pheasant population boomed. Also, I was living in a particularly good pheasant area, and over the eleven seasons Heidi and I hunted together, I was able to spend more time afield than I had during previous years.

Heidi saw a lot of birds and it showed. She had over seventeen hundred productive points on pheasants over her career, despite sharing the hunting duties in every season except one with other dogs. During the six years she was in her prime, she made over thirteen hundred points and had just shy of five hundred roosters shot over her.

I like to think of Heidi as one of those professional boxers that corner men love. During all those seasons of hard hunting, over the thousands of miles she covered, she never suffered serious injury or illness.

In 1991, her pointer kennelmate, Rebel, died just as the season was to start. In addition to Heidi, my only other dog at the time was Gwen, a Gordon setter pup not yet six months old. Heidi carried the entire load that season, often hunting several hours a day for several days in a row. She had as good an ability to pace herself as I've ever seen in a dog. That was the year my hunting partners and I nicknamed her "The Iron Lady."

A few years ago, I was in South Dakota with my friend Joe Furrow, a shorthair breeder, on an early-season hunt for prairie chickens and sharptails. Over steaks one night with a group of hunters, many of whom were North American Versatile Hunting Dog Association members and owned titled dogs, the discussion turned to pheasants and, ultimately, to who had the best pheasant dog. Many candidates for the honor were suggested and debated, but Joe pointed to me and said, "That man had the best pheasant dog I've ever seen, bar none!"

Joe is a very plain-spoken guy and a dog man of long experience. Although I'd heard others call Heidi the best they'd ever seen, I was especially proud to hear it from him, in the company of people who had seen some very fine dogs.

The discussion took place the year I retired Heidi. Her hearing was almost gone, and she was suffering from arthritis.

She became a full-time pensioner and house dog. I wondered how she'd adjust, and whether she'd go nuts when she saw me getting ready to hunt. But she took retirement with the same dignity with which she had handled pheasants all of her career. It was as if she knew it was time to pass the torch to her daughter Blitz, who had been her understudy for the previous four seasons.

Pointing Dogs and Running Birds

One additional factor that has to be considered where pointing dogs are concerned is the pheasant's well-known tendency to be an elusive runner. Just how does a pointing dog handle these tricky birds?

The number of productive points my dogs give me on pheasants are impressive, but many of those come on hens. Roosters will hold for a point too, but because many of the ones that do so end up in someone's game pouch, the birds that run or flush wild rather than sitting tight are the ones that live to breed and pass their habits on to their offspring.

If you shoot roosters only over solid points, you will pass up quite a few good chances at killable birds. Pheasants often flush for no apparent reason, whether or not there's a dog anywhere near them. And when a rooster is running, a pointing dog may make a succession of unproductive points before it manages to corner the bird. Or, at least as likely, the bird will take wing without the dog ever pinning it.

Once I know that my dog is a reliable, staunch pointer, I tend to give him the benefit of the doubt. If he's working a bird that flushes some distance from him but gives me a good shot, I'll take it. I'm operating on the assumption that the bird would have flushed anyhow, even if the dog had pointed it from fifty yards away. I've seen that happen often enough.

That said, I'd suggest some caution when following this rule with a younger, inexperienced pointing dog. If you shoot too many "wild flushes" before a dog has experience on ring-necks, he may get the idea that he doesn't have to bother pointing birds. It's a bit of a balancing act. If birds are flushing wild in spite of a youngster's best efforts and a good shot presents itself, I'll probably take it just to reward the dog for giving it his best on a tough day. However, I'd be much less likely to do the same thing on a second bird.

You should also give serious consideration to hunting a young dog without either canine or human partners during his first season. A youngster can get lazy and do nothing more than follow an older dog around. And if the veteran has some bad habits, a pup can learn things you'd rather he didn't. Another hunter is sometimes acceptable if he understands that you don't want him shooting unless your dog performs correctly. Also, even if a young dog has been properly introduced to gunfire, for his first few hunting trips you should avoid shooting directly over him, or firing too many shots too close.

Matching Your Dog to Cover and Hunting Style

Where you hunt and how you hunt are key factors to consider when mulling over what breed of dog you should own. In 1981, when I acquired my pointer Jake, he was not the best match for the covers in which I did most of my hunting. That was pre-CRP Iowa, and with the exception of some public hunting areas, there weren't many places where I could put a pointer's ability to cover ground to its best advantage.

I was teaching high school part-time then, and depending on my schedule, I could usually slip out for a quick hunt in the morning before school or in the afternoon after my last class. Jake and I spent quite a bit of time working railroad rights-of-way within a few miles of my house. And although I shot birds in those places, a big-running pointer was not the best choice for that kind of cover. (For the record, it was never actually legal to hunt railroad property. However, years ago, it was an accepted practice. Sadly, that's no longer the case. Vandalism along the tracks has caused the railroads to enforce the privacy of their rights-of-way.)

Jake was also a mismatch because of my previous experience with dogs. My first dog, a Brittany, was close working and not proficient on ringnecks. The Britt was followed by an Irish setter that wasn't proficient at anything. I wasn't used to a dog that ran as big as Jake, and he and I had to compromise on what constituted acceptable range. Unfortunately, Jake died just as the CRP was taking hold; those big fields would have been perfect for him.

From 1987 to 1997, my pointing dogs and I spent as much time as possible hunting CRP grasslands that ranged from eighty acres to almost a square mile. There were plenty of birds, and I had permission to hunt dozens of farms.

But under the 1996 Farm Bill, Washington altered the CRP, and as a result, Iowa lost about one million acres of set-aside ground. Personally, I lost roughly 90 percent of the CRP land that I had hunted for the past decade.

After 1996, the emphasis of the CRP in Iowa changed from big grasslands to buffer strips. As I mentioned in Chapter One, these strips are one-hundred-foot cover corridors on

The author's predominantly white (thus easy-to-see) English setter, Abby, points with style in heavy cover.

Heidi, a German shorthair, and Gwen, a Gordon setter, working as a team.

either side of a waterway. They are also excellent places to hunt ringnecks, but they are very different from the large CRP fields. You don't need a big-going dog to hunt buffer strips effectively. Given that many of them are planted in extremely tall, thick stands of prairie grass, where you can't see your dog on point and where you might not be able to shoot if you walk in to put the bird in flight, a strong case can be made for a flushing dog. The flushing breeds—spaniels and retrievers— are also more proficient at recovering downed birds than are pointing dogs. And when you drop a rooster in the thick stuff you find in many of the buffer strips, you need a good retriever.

Thus, from the standpoint of matching dog to cover, I would have been better off with a flushing dog when I got Jake. And I would be better off with one now, at least in most of the places I hunt. But in the interim, I became so accustomed to hunting behind pointing dogs and so enamored with the idea of shooting birds over points that I'm not likely to change. However, I'll stick with my shorthairs or another close-working pointing breed rather than going back to a wide-ranging pointer.

Before the 1999 season, I picked up a little English setter named Abby that I'd seen while quail hunting in Texas. She was a great dog, not as big-running as Jake had been, but very quick and fast on her feet. Her points, with the much-touted "twelve o'clock tail," were something to see.

If only I had owned Abby a decade earlier! She was great in the few remaining CRP fields, but not nearly as efficient as my shorthairs along ditches, waterways, fencerows—the long, narrow "strip" cover where I now do much of my hunting. We hunted together for two seasons, and she gave me some great moments when I could put her down in the right kind of cover. After I lost her in a tragic accident, I went back to my shorthairs and Gordon setter, who were better matches for the places we did most of our pheasant chasing.

Once again, let me caution you to beware of breed generalizations. There are many shorthairs that range farther than the majority of pheasant hunters would find comfortable. And while I've yet to see a really close-working pointer, Jake was deadly on cripples, a skill that runs counter to the pointer's reputation as a retriever.

Another point is that you should think of matching your choice of dog not only to the cover you hunt, but also to how you prefer to hunt and to what overall style makes you most comfortable. If you want a dog that's always within gun range, then a flushing breed may be best for you. But with a bit of looking, you can find pointing dogs that are also close workers. My Gordon setter, for example, probably spent more time hunting within gun range than she did beyond.

Pointing Labrador retrievers seem to be a current fad with pheasant hunters. Labs have always been popular pheasant dogs, primarily because they're excellent retrievers, so why not one that points?

Pointing-dog people will tell you that the advantage of the various pointing breeds is that they cover more ground than the flushers, and when they find a bird, they point it rather than flush it. Theoretically, a hunter can see his charge locked up several hundred yards away, stroll leisurely to the dog, then flush and shoot the rooster it has pinned for him. However, it usually it doesn't turn out that way with pheasants, which can be less patient than other gamebirds about waiting around for the guy with the gun. But sometimes it works as we imagine it, and then it's really neat.

Thus, if you have a dog that always stays within gun range, like Labradors typically do, there's not much advantage to a point other than offering somewhat more advance notice than you get with a standard flush.

Although pointing-Labrador people say that their dogs run bigger than traditional flushing retrievers, Labs can't compete with the pointing breeds for speed and range. They just aren't built for it. It's like giving a football to an offensive lineman and expecting him to do what a running back does.

So what you end up with is a close-working pointing dog that's an excellent retriever. Nothing wrong with that, but at least where I hunt, if I had a Lab, I'd rather it flushed. When my dogs go on point in thick, buffer-strip cover, I frankly admit to moments of "flusher envy." I have to wade into the tall, dense prairie grass, find the dog (which can be tough even with a beeper collar), then be able to shoot. On the other hand, many of my strip covers are narrow enough that if I had a flusher working in them and birds came up, I'd probably have open shots from outside the thick stuff. Even though I love to shoot birds over points, if I ever get a Labrador, it will be one that flushes.

Beware of Titles

Something else you need to beware of when considering dog breeds is the meaning of the word "champion." If your pup's pedigree refers to champions in the family tree, especially the parents, you want to know whether they are show or field champions. Although a few dogs earn both titles, such dual champions are uncommon.

Some breeds have clear splits between show dogs and field dogs. Three popular hunting breeds that show such a division are the golden retriever, English setter, and English springer spaniel. Dogs from show bloodlines may turn into decent hunters, but the odds aren't in your favor. Look for animals out of solid stock from breeders who produce working gun dogs, field-trial dogs, or both.

You may also want to steer clear of certain lines of field-trial dogs, again depending on your needs and your comfort level. Some pointing dogs, especially pointers and English setters, compete in open-country trials where their handlers follow them on horseback. These are big-running dogs. If you hunt pheasants where your dog can cut loose and cover ground—for example, in some of the Western states—that style may be what you want. Conversely, it may not work for you if you do most of your hunting in smaller, thicker cover.

Other pointing dogs run in National Shoot to Retrieve Association trials, American Kennel Club hunting tests, or, in the case of the versatile breeds (shorthairs, wirehairs, etc.), participate in testing under the auspices of the North American Versatile Hunting Dog Association. In general, these dogs will be closer working than those that run in horseback trials.

Retriever championships typically have to do with water-fowling skills, not upland hunting ability. You can pay a lot of money for a Labrador pup out of field-champion breeding, and it may come from parents that don't hunt pheasants at all. That's not to say that a well-bred waterfowl retriever can't, or won't, hunt pheasants. But if you want a Labrador, golden, or Chesapeake Bay retriever for upland work, I'd suggest looking at offspring of dogs that have been doing it for generations.

With the spaniels, you can pretty much count on their trials and tests as an accurate measure of hunting ability in the field.

Breed Differences in the Field

In spaniel field trials, the dogs are required to "Hup" (spaniel lingo for sit) when a bird flushes. In a broad sense, "Hup" is the flusher's equivalent of the pointing dog's "Whoa" command. And just as a well-trained pointing dog should stop to a verbal "Whoa," so should a spaniel sit to a verbal "Hup." If you have a hard-going springer spaniel hot on the trail of a running rooster, the dog may get beyond gun range in his excitement—at which point he's no good to you. Giving

Labradors are very popular in pheasant country because they are competent, close-working hunters and excellent retrievers.

him a "Hup" will allow you to catch up. This is also a safety measure that keeps the dog out of your line of fire. Trained flushing dogs are taught to "Hup" at a bird's flight and to stay down at the shot. And it's especially important with spaniels, because they're so eager to get the birds that they'll often jump in an attempt to grab a flushing rooster. Retrievers used as flushers aren't always taught this command (when they are, "Sit" not "Hup" is used), but for the most part they aren't as hard-charging after birds as are spaniels.

With the pointing breeds, a dog should be stationary after locating a bird. The gunner may have to move in front to flush the rooster, thus accidental shootings are somewhat less likely than with flushers. Some field trials require pointing dogs to be "steady" to wing and shot—that is, not moving from their point at either the flush or the shot. Like spaniels, they are trained to wait for a command from their owner. This can also be a safety issue.

However, I do not train my dogs to be steady, because I don't want them to lose precious time getting to a downed bird. Seconds can often make the difference between a crippled rooster that escapes and one the dog recovers. I can't recall a single instance when one of my dogs pursuing a flying bird has kept me from shooting. I'm usually closer to the bird when it departs than they are, which is seldom the case with hunters who use flushers. But a concerned pointing-dog owner always has the option to train his dog to be steady.

To summarize, if you're most comfortable hunting with a dog that seldom strays beyond gun range, a well-bred and well-trained spaniel or flushing retriever is the right choice. The primary spaniel and retrieving breeds are very strong at recovering downed birds, which is a real plus to a pheasant hunter. If you spend most of your time hunting in smaller patches of relatively thick cover, a spaniel or a retriever is an excellent choice.

If you hunt bigger, more open cover, such as large CRP fields or prairie grasslands, you may want to select one of the pointing breeds. Although you'll find great variation in the range at which pointing dogs hunt—remember, they spend most of their time beyond gun range—you can pick a close-, medium-, or wide-ranging dog by carefully selecting breed and bloodline. You're more likely to get a bigger-going pointer or English setter than you are a Brittany or one of the versatile breeds such as a German shorthair or wirehair, although there are Britts and versatiles that will hunt a quarter-mile or more from their handler. In general, the pointing breeds are not as good in the retrieving department as are the flushers. Within the pointing breeds, versatile hunting dogs and Brittanys are usually better at retrieving than pointers and setters.

If you haven't had much experience with bird dogs, you may be more comfortable with a spaniel or retriever. A pointing dog hunting well beyond gun range can try the "comfort level" of the novice, who may fear that the dog will flush birds out of range—which he will indeed do, if he doesn't point!

A flushing dog is somewhat easier to train for basic bird work than is a pointing dog. As long as a flusher stays within gun range and recovers downed birds, he's going to provide valuable assistance. Pointing dogs need more initial contact with birds in order to learn to point staunchly and reliably. And in some cases, turning them into good retrievers will require considerable effort.

Pup, Started Dog, or Finished Dog

The usual assumption is that you're going to start with a pup and turn him into a finished hunter. That's possible—if you are willing to commit the necessary time and effort—and there are a lot of good books and videotapes available to help you. But if you hit a snag, you may find yourself turning to the services of a professional trainer. The pro will probably charge you at least $400 per month. When you add this to the $400 to $600 (or more) you paid for the pup, you quickly reach $1,500 to $2,000. In my part of the country, that amount of money will buy you a well-started dog. No matter what the breed, such a dog will have been exposed to quite a few birds and should know the basics of finding, pointing or flushing, and retrieving them. I've owned three dogs that I bought started, and all of them turned out to be excellent hunters. One was Heidi, the best pheasant finder I've ever owned.

If you want to pay more, and we're talking thousands of dollars here, you can get a professionally finished dog that does it all. In my opinion, however, anyone who spends much time afield can turn a well-started dog into a effective partner just by hunting.

One of the advantages of buying either a started or finished dog is that you can see exactly what it knows and can do. In fact, you should insist on a full demonstration in the field, with birds, before you write a check. With a pup, you're saving money on the initial purchase, but you're also buying nothing but potential.

Reading Your Dog's Behavior

If you're going to get the most out of hunting with any

dog, whether flusher or pointer, you need to understand what the dog's telling you by its actions and body language. This is commonly called "reading your dog."

On the surface, it seems pretty simple. A pointing dog stops and points when it finds birds. Conversely, a flushing dog gets very animated, with increased tail wagging, snuffling, and speed, when it's getting close to a bird. But it's a good bit more complex than that, and different dogs have different ways of indicating what they're up to.

When pointing dogs strike scent suddenly, the reaction is usually simple and straightforward—a point with few preliminaries. But because pheasants are notorious runners, there may be quite a time lapse between when the dog first picks up scent and when he finally points the bird, assuming he succeeds in doing so.

Of the dogs I've owned, my pointers and setters have been more inclined to give me nonproductive points—a point with no bird—than my other breeds. What it means is that a bird has been at the spot the dog indicated, probably quite recently, but has moved on. When trailing a running bird, my pointer Rebel would give me a series of points. I'd think, "Aha, she's finally got that son of a gun." Then, about the time I'd reach her, she'd look over her shoulder at me—a sure signal she didn't have the bird—dash ahead fifty to one hundred yards, and point again. Eventually, if we were fortunate, the bird would decide to sit it out and I'd walk up on the point with no backward glance from the dog. But this procedure was hard on my nerves.

My shorthairs, in contrast, seem less inclined to point unless a bird is really there. What they will often do on a running bird is what I call a moving point. The dogs may stop briefly, but once they determine the bird has moved on, they'll follow the scent, stiff-legged and head thrust forward. In time, they may end up with a hard point and offer me a chance at a rooster. At least for me, this procedure is less nerve-racking than the point-dash-point maneuver.

Some pointing dog owners insist that once their dogs have established point, they not move until given a verbal or physical release command (like a tap on the head) to relocate and follow the bird. Having worked a lot of pheasants as they zigzagged through CRP fields, I'm more comfortable allowing a dog to relocate on its own. However, this can cause problems with birds that absolutely refuse to hold, and with dogs that lose their patience.

A buddy and I were chasing pheasants—and I do mean chasing, on this particular day—in a large, grassy field. Normally one would expect the birds to hold well in such cover, but for whatever reason even the hens were nervous that day. Blitz, a veteran with seasons of experience behind her, was reaching the edge of exasperation. She'd point, relocate, point, trail, and point again, only to have the bird flush well beyond gun range. Reading her actions, I knew the birds were serious runners.

After several of these sequences, I saw her hit a hard point about one hundred yards away, and figured she'd finally managed to nail one. Because the birds weren't holding, I called to my buddy that we needed to get there as quickly as possible.

We'd covered maybe fifty yards when I saw Blitz's point soften just a bit. Then she took several bounds through the cover, stopped briefly, and did the same thing again. She almost caught the rooster on her last jump. I was just as frustrated as the dog, and I shot at the bird to no effect.

After a bunch of birds had run out from under her points, apparently she decided to catch one of the slippery rascals. The pheasants weren't playing by the rules that day, so neither would she.

Breaking point isn't preferred behavior, but you have to read your dog and sometimes make allowances, even for a veteran, if the birds are really giving him a hard time.

When a flusher or pointer is pushing a running bird too fast, what a handler can do is command "Hup" or "Whoa" to stop the dog and remind him that he not only needs to find birds, but also needs to do so under control.

Control and Electronic Collars

Control of your dog can be hard to maintain on pheasants, as I illustrated above, because the birds would usually rather run than fly. They can lead a dog on a merry chase, and while the dog needs to follow if you're to get a shot, he must do it with a measure of restraint.

In training, you can teach control with a check cord and, in time, have your dog conditioned to "Hup" or "Whoa" on command. The electronic collar, or e-collar—commonly called a shock collar—is another training device that will help you establish control. Some hunters use them in the field as a tangle-free "electronic check cord."

An e-collar probably would have made my first pheasant dog into a much more effective partner. As I said earlier, I brought Deke back from Morocco, where he'd been a reliable pointer and retriever of quail and partridge. He worked equally well in this country on woodcock, grouse, and bobwhites.

Pheasants were another story. Deke and I hunted together in the pre-CRP mid-1970s, working fencerows, ditches, water-ways, and other similar covers. A lot of the birds ran and Deke would follow them under control for a ways, but he didn't have much patience for their games. He'd usually look back at me with frustration, and when he did I knew what was going to happen. He'd take off and eventually catch up with the bird, almost always out of gun range, and because he was pushing hard, the bird would seldom hold for a point. The result was a lot of yelling, whistle-blowing, and long-range flushes.

We went back to check-cord work, but Deke would always backslide after he encountered a running bird or two. He'd obey "Whoa" if he was within check-cord range of maybe fifty feet, but once he was farther away, he knew I had no way of stopping him. If I had had an e-collar then, I'm confident I could have cured that problem.

I got my first e-collar shortly after I acquired Jake, my first really good pheasant dog. It was preseason, and Jake and I were training on a public hunting area not far from home. He pointed reliably when he found pheasants, but on this partic-ular day the pheasants weren't holding. There was a large field of unpicked corn on one edge of the public area, and that's where the birds—and Jake—headed. He got into the corn-stalk jungle and didn't come out. He was lost for several days, but I got him back when a farmer spotted the "lost dog" note I'd left in a local cafe.

With the e-collar, Jake learned that pheasants or no pheas-ants, he wasn't supposed to go where the boss didn't want him to go. I also used the e-collar to shorten his range. Even though I was doing a lot of running then, I had trouble keeping up with him. He'd get out of sight quickly and before long I'd lose the sound of his bell. Because I prefer to hunt for birds and not dogs, we worked on that situation until we reached an agreement. Once we did, we became an effective team.

Electronic collars have gotten much better since I bought my first one in the early 1980s. They now have variable stimulation-intensity levels, controlled from a handheld transmitter. On most modern units, you can scarcely feel the lowest level, but it may be enough to remind Rover that he needs to listen to the boss. My old e-collar had just one level—high.

Many of the new e-collars combine the stimulation feature with a beeper that is also controlled from the transmitter. If you're hunting where you can see your dog most of the time, you can leave the beeper off. If the dog goes into heavy cover, you can activate it to keep track of him. The beeps go from slow to fast if the dog stops. This is the "point" mode, which will lead you to a dog that's located a bird or, if you're less fortunate, to one that's stopped to do its business. Most beepers also offer a "point only" option, which means that the dog runs silently, but the beeper activates automatically when he stops.

Some people believe that e-collars ruin more dogs than they benefit, and should be used only by professionals. Undeniably, a heavy jolt of electricity is powerful medicine. However, you can avoid trouble if you follow the directions that come with all electronic training units, and use a ration of common sense when dispensing correction. But if you're likely to lose your cool and take it out on the dog if he misbehaves, you can run into problems using an e-collar.

The beauty of the e-collar is that you can correct a dog as

it is in the process of disobeying a command. You should never use stimulation until your dog understands and responds to particular commands. But once he knows what you expect, electricity is an excellent tool, both in training and in the field.

Prior to the advent of the e-collar, your options to correct a dog that disobeyed, especially at some distance from you, were limited. You could try to run the dog down and punish him. If you called him in (assuming he responded) and you then punished him, he might have associated the punishment with responding to your "Come" command rather than with the command that he disobeyed. You could go back to square one and train again on whatever command he didn't obey, but like my experience with Deke, there was no guarantee that what worked in training would also work in the field.

Whether you hunt your dog with an e-collar or not is a personal choice. Because I now have one of the stimulation-beeper combinations, my dogs wear it frequently, though mainly for the beeper feature. However, the stimulation unit is always there and available in case a correction needs to be made.

You can also use the e-collar as a means of preventing unwanted or dangerous behavior. Let's say that your dog is tempted to chase a deer. If he's never seen one in training, you may have trouble stopping him. But I've broken dogs off deer-chasing with just one push of the transmitter button. Last year in South Dakota, my young shorthair Donner made a beautiful point—on a jackrabbit. When he took off in pursuit, he discovered that the hare was shocking. He pointed the next jack he found as well, but when it took off, he just looked at me as if to say, "I'm not messing with those any more!" Later that year, while hunting quail in New Mexico, we encountered numerous jackrabbits, some of which jumped right under Donner's nose, but he did not chase a single hare.

In Iowa, it's legal to hunt the road ditches that provide some of the best pheasant cover around. But I'll hunt those ditches only on secondary, gravel roads, usually using my veteran Blitz, and I'll put the e-collar on her as an extra measure of control for her safety along roadways.

However you establish and maintain it, control of your hunting dog is critical. A dog that's under control is a benefit to you; one that's out of control will ruin a hunt and fray your nerves.

Is it still possible to hunt pheasants without a dog? Yes, but in my opinion you won't do it very effectively. If you don't have a dog, the only birds you will find are the ones that sit tight, and therefore you must choose your cover carefully. Fencerows, narrow road ditches, and waterways are where you should concentrate your efforts. Walk slowly and pause frequently; many of your flushes will come when you're stopped. And pick your shots carefully, because recovering downed roosters is much tougher without a dog.

The best advice I can give a dogless hunter is to get a dog or hunt with someone who has one. It won't take you long to realize that a decent dog makes you a much more effective pheasant hunter.

But effectiveness in the field is not the sole reason—perhaps not even the primary reason—why pheasant hunting should be done by a human-dog team. In our increasingly urban world, we spend most of our time working with other people or, more and more these days, with machines. Hunting remains one of the few pursuits in which we can participate with another species of animal. The man-dog relationship, which has existed for thousands of years, has a way of taking the human half of the team back in time to when it was really necessary to hunt for food to survive. I find this link with our past to be an intriguing and refreshing aspect of the sport.

Apart, man and dog are inefficient hunters. A man can kill birds, but his weak senses give him a poor chance of locating them. A dog can locate birds, but without assistance he stands a poor chance of killing them. Together, man and dog make a perfect hunting team.

When you, as the more intelligent member of this team, watch a dog unravel a pheasant's scent trail, using a sense of smell thousands of times keener than your own, you will feel as if you are watching a miracle unfold. If you spend much time hunting with a dog, you will soon learn why many experienced hunters say that they would rather go afield without a gun than without their dog.

SIX

Where to Hunt Pheasants

Obviously, you must have access to good cover in order to be a successful pheasant hunter. In my opinion, good cover ranks right up there with good dogs and good shooting as key factors in bagging pheasants.

But what is good pheasant cover? There is no single answer to that question. It depends on the topography of the region you hunt, the major crops in your area, the weather, and even the time of day.

Finding cover that holds pheasants isn't the only problem. Once you've found good habitat, you have to hunt it effectively. That depends not only on the features of cover itself, but also on the composition of your hunting party. For example, what is the size of the party, and do the members have any particular strengths or weaknesses as individuals or as a group that will make them more or less effective in particular habitats? How many dogs do you have, and in what kind of cover do they work best?

Getting Permission to Hunt

You can't always select ideal cover because you have to

155

Always get landowner permission and instructions on where to hunt if you're working private land. The landowner may also be able to tell you where he's seen birds.

hunt what is available to you. Pheasant hunting in most areas requires gaining access to private land. Therefore, what is available to you depends on your ability to get landowner permission to hunt.

As I mentioned in Chapter Two, going afield on opening day in a heavily hunted area requires that you make your arrangements well in advance. Remember, too, that obtaining permission tends to get easier as the season wears on and the number of hunters thins out. Finally, landowners are more likely to give permission to one or two hunters they don't know than to an entire gang of unknowns.

I doubt that I'd make much of a salesman, because I'm not comfortable knocking on doors and asking permission. But

I've gotten better at it over the years. For me, the direct approach seems to be the best.

I start by introducing myself and telling the landowner where I live. Then I ask if the particular piece of ground I'm interested in hunting belongs to him. (Often, I'll be operating from a county plat book and will have a good idea of who owns what before I ask.) If he replies in the affirmative, I ask if he'd mind me hunting there.

A good 80 to 90 percent of the time I get permission using this straightforward approach. When I do get turned down, the landowner usually gives me a good reason. He may have livestock that I didn't see in his fields, or he may reserve hunting rights for friends and relatives. If the latter is the case, the farmer will often invite me to return later in the season.

If I get permission, I ask the landowner where his property stops and the neighbor's starts. I avoid trespassing at all costs, and most landowners will have a higher opinion of a responsible hunter who makes sure he is hunting where he belongs. A secondary advantage of this question is that it may reveal other parcels of good bird cover I hadn't spotted.

Once I've found out where I can hunt, I ask the landowner if he enjoys a pheasant dinner. Most farm families do, but few farmers have time for bird hunting. Typically, I tell the landowner that I'll be happy to share my good fortune with him. I always follow through on this promise, though most of the time I don't drop off birds immediately after a hunt. Unless the landowner indicates that he prefers to dress the birds himself, I believe in sharing cleaned game with my host. I'd rather take the birds home, clean them properly, and drop off a couple of frozen roosters on my next trip.

I prefer doing it this way for a couple of reasons. First, I may have collected roosters that are badly shot up. I save those for myself and give less damaged birds to landowners. Also, waiting gives you an excuse for a return trip. There are few landowners, especially if they have given you permission once already, who will turn you down if you show up on their doorstep with a couple of birds for them.

I continue to be amazed at the number of places I hunt—most with excellent cover and good bird numbers—where no other hunter has offered to share his bag with the landowner. In a normal season I give away far more pheasants than I keep.

This simple and cost-free way of saying thank you has cemented a number of continuing relationships with landowners. By way of example, there is a widow who lives near me who is a regular recipient on my "pheasant delivery route." She owns one hundred and sixty acres that at one time included a nice piece of CRP land that has unfortunately reverted to crop production. Even after I stopped hunting her farm, I continued to drop by with a couple of birds for her. On one stop, I inquired about the farm across the road, a quarter-section with some excellent cover but no house. It turned out that the owner was her nephew, who didn't live nearby. She called him on my behalf and obtained permission for me to hunt there whenever I choose to do so. I still haven't met the nephew, but now I drop off extra birds for him and always ask the widow to convey my thanks to the man.

On another occasion, I planned to hunt a piece of CRP land some distance from my home. My partner that day was a local who had secured permission from the landowner. We had just unloaded the dogs when a truck came bouncing across the field. The driver was the man who lived in the house that was surrounded by the property we were about to hunt. He neither owned nor farmed the ground, but he was unhappy that we hadn't bothered to stop and check with him. We smoothed his ruffled feathers and went on with our hunt.

A month or so later, I was hunting alone in the same area. I had a couple of birds with me that I'd intended to drop off with a farmer I knew, but no one was home. I wasn't far from the place my partner and I had hunted previously, so I decided to swing by. I found the fellow at home, and when I handed him the birds he lit up like a one-hundred-watt bulb. Not only were there no more ruffled feathers, but from then on I was welcomed at his place like a long-lost cousin. In fact, he told me that the owner had another farm nearby that I could also hunt—the owner had given him the control of access. He became a regular pheasant delivery customer, and I had two more farms that I've now hunted for several years.

Hunters make different kinds of gifts to farmers. A Wisconsin friend offers a selection of his state's fine cheeses. Other friends have given landowners a bottle of good scotch, which works fine as long as you're not dealing with a teetotaler. The important thing is to thank the landowner sincerely, and I feel that something tangible reinforces my gratitude. Sharing your game with a farmer seems especially appropriate. After all, he provides the food and shelter that sustain the pheasants.

How about offering money? I'd suggest you proceed carefully here. In some places, payment of a "trespass fee" is considered standard procedure. In South Dakota, for example, it's not unusual to shell out at least fifty dollars per hunter per day for access to land with good cover and plenty of birds. In Iowa, on the other hand, you may offend a landowner if you offer cash. There is some leasing of hunting rights on private ground, but paying a trespass fee is uncommon.

When you are hunting a new area, one of the best ways to find good cover is through a local contact who is also a pheasant hunter. He will not only have access to private ground, but most likely it will be good cover. Nonhunting contacts may introduce you to farmer friends of theirs and think that they are doing you a big favor when the only cover available to hunt is a couple of blades of grass in the middle of a bare pasture.

If you're doing a lot of hunting in one or two counties, plat books—I referred to them earlier—are invaluable resources. You can get them at the appropriate county courthouse. They show property boundaries and list owners, addresses, and telephone numbers.

These days,one of the real problems for nonlocals seeking pheasant cover is that land ownership patterns have changed. Twenty years ago, it was a pretty safe assumption that someone who lived on a piece of ground owned and farmed it. With fewer and fewer farmers working more and more ground in order to stay in business, that's no longer the case.

For example, I live on a one-hundred-and-sixty-acre farm, but I own only the two acres immediately surrounding my house. If someone were to stop and ask me for permission to hunt, I'd have to tell them that the owner lives in Florida, and the farmer who rents the ground lives several miles away.

I can hunt the three hundred and twenty acres just west of my place, as well as another one hundred and twenty acres about five miles away. Both pieces of land are owned by the same farmer. But neither he nor a renter lives on either farm, which means you'd have a tough time running down the land's owner without a plat book.

Another problem is catching landowners at home. A couple of decades ago, you'd typically find the farm wife at home, if not the landowner himself. These days, many farm wives have jobs in town. Around noon is always a good time to check, because the farmer may be grabbing some lunch. Otherwise, your best chances of making contact are early in the morning—but not too early, because all farmers don't get up at the crack of dawn—or in the evening.

Although the plat book will give you the landowner's telephone number, I would advise not calling until you have met him first. Most landowners like to look you in the eye and size you up before they give you permission to hunt. Once you've met them, follow-up phone calls are fine.

Evaluating Pheasant Cover

To my way of thinking, trying to interpret a pheasant's daily schedule is not a good way to evaluate and select huntable cover. If you watch pheasants before the season, you will see that they are indeed birds of habit, moving out to feed at about the same time every day unless severe weather interrupts this pattern. However, pheasants adapt to pressure from hunters. The birds feed when they can and spend the rest of their time avoiding two-legged predators.

There are exceptions to this rule of thumb, but in general once the season has been under way for a couple of weeks and the birds have been exposed to hunting pressure, their daily schedules are no longer reliable.

Most of the time, you will have to find your own hunting spots. One way to locate good cover is to look for the pheasant's preferred food supply. In my part of the country, pheasants relate closely to corn, which not only makes up much of their diet during the hunting season, but also provides excellent cover until it has been harvested.

That said, when I look at standing corn, I have the same reaction as Indiana Jones faced with a room full of snakes. I hate standing corn. It encourages birds to run and dogs to chase them. And getting good shots in the midst of a forest of seven-foot stalks is tough. Although I avoid standing corn whenever I can, sometimes it's not possible to do so. The beginning of the 1997 season offers a good example.

We got hit by a blizzard on the second day of the season. The storm was memorable for two reasons. First, my partner and I shot quick limits that day—roosters were hunkered down and holding tight in heavy cover. Second, 1997 was a late-harvest year. It was also my last season guiding pheasant hunters, and with all my normal CRP covers buried under a blanket of white, I had to hunt standing corn to get clients into birds.

Gwen, my Gordon setter, saw more action that year than she did during my other three guiding seasons combined. She wasn't very effective on CRP land because she didn't cover a lot of ground. But that weakness, and the fact she didn't like to lose track of me, became a strength in standing corn. She worked close, pointed birds that tried to run out the sides or hold tight when we reached the end of the rows, and did a nice job of retrieving. It was an excellent example of matching dog to the cover available.

Once the snow had melted and the corn had been harvested, I shifted my focus to the CRP fields I preferred. And Gwen shifted from first-string dog back to third string, behind my mother-daughter shorthair team of Heidi and Blitz. Even as a twelve-year-old that season, Heidi covered more ground than Gwen who was half her age. And four-year-old Blitz was in her prime, running those fields like her mother had in her younger days.

From the mid-1980s through 1997, I spent most of my time hunting CRP fields. In 1989, for example, thirty-five of the sixty-three roosters I shot were taken from block CRP cover. With the exception of the hunts in standing corn at the beginning of the 1997 season, my focus remained on the large blocks of CRP land through the end of the year.

Comparing my 1989 season results with those of 2001 makes a useful point. In 2001, I shot almost the same number of birds (sixty) as I did in 1989 (sixty-three), but only twelve of them came from big CRP fields. I took forty-seven roosters from some sort of "strip" cover—CRP buffer strips,waterways, ditches, and fencerows. The sixtieth bird came out of picked corn.

When an old criminal was asked why he robbed banks, he replied, "Because that's where the money is!" I shifted cover types with the same basic idea in mind: I went where the birds were. There were several reasons for this shift.

First, as I have already mentioned, between 1991 and 1998 Iowa lost half of its total CRP land, dropping from about two million acres to just over a million. Second, the CRP emphasis switched from large blocks of cover to the "buffer strip" configuration that I described in Chapter One. Finally, when I did hunt in block CRP during 2001, I simply did not

Heavy cover such as this grassy field is a good place to look for cold-weather birds.

find many birds. The areas where I was having my best luck were characterized by strip cover.

Nesting cover and winter cover are two factors that can have a significant impact on pheasant populations. In Iowa, until the hard winter of 2000, we had escaped bad weather for quite a few years. But nesting cover had been a limiting factor since a majority of Iowa farmers switched to intensive row-crop agriculture in the 1960s and 1970s.

The CRP restored critical nesting cover not only in Iowa but throughout much of the Midwest. Where the birds had few places to nest in the spring of 1986, hundreds of thousands of acres were available in 1987. The result was a dramatic surge in pheasant numbers.

Iowa pheasant hunting remained good through the 2000 season, even though we'd lost much of our CRP land a few

Big Conservation Reserve Program fields, such as the one pictured here, can hold roosters, but it takes a dog to find them.

years earlier. Mother Nature was relatively kind to us with decent winters and nesting seasons. But Iowa birds were living on borrowed time. The best pheasant numbers were in the northern tier of the state, which lost most of its CRP acreage during the late 1990s. When we finally did get hit with a hard winter, the bottom dropped out of the pheasant population. With the exception of pieces of northern Iowa habitat immediately adjacent to state-owned or restored wetlands, where the birds could find decent cover, that part of the state suffered significant losses.

Southern Iowa, on the other hand, hadn't lost nearly as much CRP land. Unfortunately, there were other problems in that region of the state. Springs had been either too wet or too dry and resulted in poor nesting success. And in some areas, so much land had been taken out of agricultural production that quality food—primarily corn and soybeans—was not readily available.

But assuming good pheasant numbers, large CRP or grass fields are areas that I still love to hunt. Give me one of these fields—forty acres if it's small, up to a half-section if it's big—and I can count on my dogs to find birds.

An ideal CRP or grass field has cover that is tall enough and thick enough to hide the birds, yet not so dense that they can't run in it. Most of the time it's not especially hard walking. I certainly prefer it to slogging through a marsh or slinking between rows of standing corn.

Hunters accustomed to working narrower, less imposing pieces of cover may be intimidated by large CRP fields. But unlike enormous blocks of standing corn, CRP ground does not require an army of hunters. Although in some cases (especially late in the season) several hunters may be more effective, a lone hunter with a good dog can do well in this kind of cover.

Initially, one's reaction is that the birds can be anywhere in cover that big. While pheasants do have a lot of options in many of these fields, I find that they prefer certain areas within what at first appears to be a relatively featureless ocean of cover. If you hunt most larger CRP fields three or four times, you will discover that pheasants relate to subtle variations in cover: a shift from one type of grass to another, an old ditch or fenceline, a slight change in elevation.

For example, during the 2001 season, I took two roosters from one small (under forty acres) patch of CRP cover on two successive visits. The birds flushed within fifty yards of each

Small pockets of cover, such as abandoned, overgrown farmsteads, will often hold birds.

other, from a draw between two small hills where the vegetation was a bit heavier than on the rest of the area.

But even by focusing on these preferred "mini-habitats," you are not likely to find many birds without canine assistance. Except perhaps on opening day, if you happen to hit one of the smaller CRP fields that holds plenty of birds and you have a lot of hunters, your chances of successfully working this kind of cover dogless are minimal.

How do you tell a good CRP field from a bad one, if indeed there is such a thing? Although the majority of this kind of cover in good pheasant country will hold birds, some set-aside fields are much better bets than others. Assuming two CRP fields with equal potential for offering

167

refuge to pheasants—that is, the same quality of tall, dense grass cover—any difference in bird numbers will usually be defined by the cover types found adjacent to the fields. One grass field surrounded by a number of other grass fields is not likely to act as a pheasant magnet. Likewise, such a field surrounded by short-grass pasture or woodlands with no crops in the vicinity does not have much potential.

But if you can locate a block of CRP ground—I prefer at least eighty acres—with little other good bird-holding cover but with plenty of crops in the vicinity, in all likelihood you've found the ringneck version of El Dorado. Once again, as I mentioned, you should always look for a food supply. In this case, the birds are not living right in their kitchen as they do in standing corn, but they do prefer staying within strolling distance of their pantry. Let me illustrate this by following the cover changes on and surrounding one particular area that I hunted for more than a decade.

One Cover Over the Seasons

This particular piece of cover consists of two farms and totals about five hundred and sixty acres—an entire section minus eighty acres sliced off by a jog in a perimeter road. I had permission to hunt everything within the boundaries formed by gravel roads on the four sides.

The section's "permanent" cover consists of a creek that runs a mile from the property's north to its south end. Midway along the creek a little tributary forms another strip of cover a half-mile long. I first hunted the cover late in the 1985 season and shot a couple of birds that were taking refuge from the cold and deep snow in the dense creek-bank habitat.

168

In 1986, most of the ground adjacent to the creek was planted in corn. As soon as the corn was picked, the farmer turned his cattle into the field. I made one hunt on the place, and by the time I got there the cattle had stomped the cover flat.

In 1987, the smaller of the two farms on the section—one hundred and eighty acres—went into the CRP. I made eight trips to the area, hunted a total of twenty hours, and bagged twelve birds.

The surrounding cover, in the fields just across the adjacent roads, was almost perfect. There was picked corn to the north, picked grain and pasture to the east and west, pasture and a grass field to the south. Eventually, toward the end of the 1987 season, the birds began to flush wild and fly into the grass south of the road where I couldn't hunt. It was the only escape cover available.

In 1988, because of severe drought, farmers were permitted to cut hay off their CRP land, which is what happened on the smaller of the two farms. However, about eighty acres of the larger farm went into the CRP. Hunting this cover and the creek, I took four roosters in a total of six hours.

By 1989, all of the large farm except one hundred acres was in the CRP. In addition, the cover on the small farm had grown back even thicker than it had been in the two previous seasons. The surrounding cover was much like it had been in 1987, except that the grass field across the road to the south had been mowed for hay. I hunted pheasants on both farms eleven times for a total of twenty-three hours and put sixteen roosters in the bag. I also knocked down two others and lost them in the heavy cover.

169

Because the birds had a large and well-established block of excellent habitat and no surrounding escape cover, they were reluctant to leave the area. They would flush, fly some distance, then settle back into the cover. The exception to this pattern was when they were pushed up against one of the boundary roads; then they would reluctantly leave their sanctuary. On several occasions, just after shooting hours, I spotted numerous birds walking or flying back into the cover.

Over the next eight seasons, the cover on the two farms didn't change much. My partners and I shot one hundred and thirty-nine roosters off that ground, though our best year by far was 1991 when we bagged thirty. The property was consistently productive pheasant habitat, especially when you consider that I never hunted it on opening weekend.

On the opener the farms were usually reserved for a party of ten or more hunters, who almost always took limits both Saturday and Sunday, which meant that the pheasant population had been reduced by the time my dogs and I got our turn. Nevertheless, each season the farms produced birds for me.

It all came to an end in 1998. The smaller of the two farms was sold to a new owner, and as was the case in much of central Iowa, nearly all the CRP land disappeared. I hunted the bigger farm just once that year, for old times' sake, and shot one bird.

When that section was in its prime and mostly in CRP cover (from 1989 to 1997) the hunting tended to hold up well over the course of a season, from the first time I hunted it in early November to my last trip in January. When I say that the hunting remained good, I mean it in a relative sense. Although the hunting became progressively tougher, the place was never shot out.

On my first few trips to the farms, all I had to do was fol-low whichever dog I happened to be using. In 1989, my pointer Rebel produced a limit for me in a half-hour—her ground-covering speed was well suited to the habitat.

During the early part of each season, the birds did not seem to run much when pressured. The main problem was that in the normal course of moving, they left a lot of scent to be sorted out. But once the dogs got on something hot, it usu-ally wasn't long before I had a point, then a bird in the air.

But even in a big cover with a high pheasant population, you can't have it easy forever. Eventually the birds will react to pressure and to the experience they've gained through repeat-ed contacts with men, dogs, and guns.

Hunting those farms repeatedly during a decade of sea-sons taught me a lot about pheasant behavior. The birds, when they are exposed to enough pressure, will run more in heavy cover than I had previously believed. On numerous occasions, I watched one of my veteran dogs work hot scent for at least fifteen minutes, then come up empty. The pheas-ants became clever at zigzagging around the cover. Appar-ently, they learned that this was the way to thwart a dog.

On my earlier hunts, I could not have predicted where my shots might come. A bird might just as commonly flush in the middle of the section as along one of the roads, perhaps even more so. But by the end of each season, nearly all my shots would come when I pushed a bird into a corner and forced it to fly. These opportunities were all on edges of one sort or another. But even relatively late in the year, the birds seemed to follow some patterns that were fairly predictable.

One day in early December, a partner and I were hunting

in the general vicinity of the farms. We weren't having much luck, so I decided to head to my "honey hole." Unfortunately, someone was there ahead of us. It was close to noon, and after a quick lunch we tried another place a few miles away, but we found no birds.

It was now after 3 P.M., and with little more than an hour's shooting time left, I was running out of options. On a hunch, I drove back to the farm. The other hunters had departed. There was a large CRP field that ran about three-quarters-of-a-mile up the east boundary road. With the wind out of the north, I parked at the south end.

My partner eyed me skeptically. "We gonna hunt here, so soon after those other guys left?"

"The birds are almost always right along this road late in the afternoon, either going out to feed on the other side, or coming back in to roost," I replied. I could see he was still a skeptic.

The tactic worked like a charm. I turned my shorthair, Heidi, loose, and by the time my partner and I reached the far end of the property at 4:30 P.M. we had each collected a pair of roosters

Other hot spots on that property were the northwest corner, where the birds were safe if they flew (unless we had a blocker) because of the proximity of houses; the creeks and the adjacent cover, especially in nasty weather; and a depression below an old barn on the northeast corner, which was a ringneck hang-out when other parts of the farm were snowed under.

My familiarity with the farms along with their ability to produce birds on a regular basis made me particularly sad to lose the cover. Indeed, I haven't had such consistent results—

at least not season after season—from any other farm that I've hunted. Either bird numbers were down in a particular area or the habitat changed enough from year to year so that no other piece of ground remained as productive as the combination of the two farms.

Different Covers Mean Different Challenges

During the 2001 season, I started hunting a long stretch of CRP buffer strip—a mile-and-a-half all together—on a farm not far from my house. I'd hunted the waterway on that farm for a couple of years and had shot a few birds, but the buffer strips were new in 2001. I took thirteen roosters off that place, and never failed to bag at least one. And this was with the buffer-strip cover only a few inches high. When that stuff grows to its potential—well, let's say I have high hopes for it.

Wildlife biologists, while believing that CRP buffer strips are better than nothing, prefer larger CRP fields. Not only are more acres set aside for protection, but biologists say that predators are less likely to have an impact on birds occupying bigger blocks of land than on birds in the strips, which they feel can become "feeding corridors" for various critters out for a pheasant dinner.

I prefer the larger fields, too, but from what I've seen as we transition to more buffer strips and fewer fields, I suspect that the strips may be better than biologists believe. For one thing, many of the strips feature some form of prairie-grass mix, which is better cover than the shorter, less dense grass varieties (such as brome) often seen in traditional CRP fields. And the number of birds that I find in the strips, even late in the season, seems to indicate that they're faring quite well.

In general, pheasants tend to be nervous and inclined to run or flush wild in strip cover. This seems logical when you consider that they're more likely to encounter a predator—either two- or four-legged—in one of the narrow strips than they are in a quarter-section of grass. But what I'm finding in the buffer strips is that even where there's a fair amount of hunting pressure, the birds aren't necessarily dashing or flying away at the first sign of a hunter's approach. My notes from the 2001 season provide a good illustration.

It was January 5, the final weekend of the season. I was hunting a farm in southeastern Iowa that I've visited numerous times since the early 1980s. A group of nonresidents hunts the farm for the first few days of the season, but from then on it receives sporadic pressure. I'd hunted it once a month earlier and picked up a limit of birds, but I saw only one rooster in addition to the three I shot. I wasn't optimistic that this would be a red-letter day, especially since it was the end of Iowa's worst pheasant season on record.

I parked in the middle of the farm, near an old barn. Donner, my shorthair, and I started down a fencerow that widened into a waterway with good, heavy cover on both sides. I had picked up my first bird here on my previous trip. But the dog didn't even act birdy, so I swung him through a small patch of CRP cover not far below the barn. Nothing there either.

We followed a fencerow to a much larger creek with good buffer strips on either side. We worked down one side to a ford and crossed over to another small CRP field on the far side. It too was devoid of birds. Donner and I dropped back down to the creek and worked the streamside cover back to the ford.

By this time we'd been hunting for over an hour. The dog had yet to get birdy, and we hadn't seen as much as a hen.

Another small waterway fed into the creek. It ran for about a quarter-mile, up to a large dike in the middle of the field, where the cover ended.

We were about halfway up the waterway when Donner's beeper signaled "point" in the middle of a patch of especially tall and heavy grass. I took a couple of steps toward him when a big rooster came boiling up, cackling his displeasure. I dropped him hard. When Donner brought him back, it was easy to see from his long, sharp, black spurs and nearly two feet of tail that he'd survived the previous year and had almost made it through his second season.

There was a break in the cover of maybe twenty yards between the end of the buffer strips edging the small water-way and the field dike. Donner swung out around the end of the tall grass and slammed into another point. I dropped this bird as well.

I was beginning to feel good about this late-season hunt and was still admiring rooster number two when Donner hit another point, over on the far side of the waterway. But this time a couple of hens flushed.

We checked out the tall grass on the far side of the dike, but the patch of cover was birdless. From there, it was a five-minute walk across open ground to the pickup.

I was pleased that Donner's last point hadn't produced a third rooster. Blitz, his mother, hadn't had her chance yet, and there were more buffer strips to be worked on the other side of the farm.

I drove around to the far side of the property and parked

near a waterway that flowed through a culvert under a dirt road. We could go either way. I picked the west side of the road, where the waterway eventually joined the same large creek Donner and I had hunted earlier. My plan was to work down to the larger stream, check out the cover along its banks, then hunt a small triangle of CRP ground on the far side.

We never made it that far. Within fifty yards of the creek, Blitz swung into a point. When I moved in to flush, two roosters took flight, one right behind the other. There I was with two birds already in the bag and what was my best chance at a double of the entire season. I swung on the lead rooster and dropped him into the picked corn next to the waterway.

It had been spitting a rain/snow mix off and on throughout that day's hunt. As Blitz and I walked back to the truck with the last bird, the snow started to come down harder. Even our weather timing was good that day!

That entire hunt took about an hour-and-a-half. Again, I only saw four roosters, but each of them held perfectly for a point. Given the scarcity of cover on adjacent farms and that this ground had been hunted numerous times, these birds had certainly encountered hunters and dogs previously. Yet they acted much as you would expect them to act on opening day.

While this isn't the norm in buffer strips, especially those that have been hunted a few times, it does happen often enough that I'm beginning to believe that they provide good enough cover that the birds feel relatively secure. But then, I've also found tight-sitting birds in road ditches and along fencerows, both of which are far narrower than the hundred-foot-wide buffer strips.

This cut corn looks barren, but the dog has pinned a bird hiding in a nearby strip of brush.

I'd still rather hunt the big CRP fields, but I won't spend too much time mourning their passing when I can get fine late-season hunting from the buffer strips.

Hunting Pheasant Food Sources

Depending on the crops available in a given area, you can sometimes hunt pheasants right in their primary food sources. I began this book with a description of hunting in standing corn. As I said earlier in this chapter, I don't like hunting uncut corn; visibility of birds and other hunters is poor, and dogs—especially pointing dogs—are difficult to keep track of and control. Hunting cornfields after they have been harvested, however, can be a very different story.

An afternoon hunt in mid-December in 1986 provides an

177

example of how and why picked corn can be productive, even late in the season.

Dave Prine and I began our hunt by working a couple of creeks and draws. We saw plenty of birds, but they were all flushing wild. It looked like one of those days when the roosters were wearing track shoes and you need an antiaircraft gun to reach them.

Then we hit a cornfield that Dave's uncle had combined a couple of days earlier. We were hunting behind two of Dave's Labradors, working up the rows one way, turning around at the fence and moving over a few rows, then hunting back the other way.

Dave already had a couple of birds in the bag. My first shot came on a chance that stretched my old Sauer side-by-side's modified barrel for all it was worth. When Dave's old Lab, Luke, retrieved that bird for me, I saw that its tail was long enough to drag on the ground.

My next two birds came up literally right at my feet. Both shots were easy, and I had one of those memorable three-for-three days. So did Dave. I usually shoot better when I hunt with him, perhaps because he's such a good shot, and I try to avoid embarrassing myself.

Re-examining that hunt, at least three reasons explain our success. The first is that the field was recently picked and it's probable that the birds, accustomed to the safety afforded by the standing corn, simply moved back in once the combine left.

The second is that a cold front was moving in. It was sunny when we began our hunt. By the time we finished, the wind had switched around to the north, it had started spitting snow, and the temperature had dropped about ten degrees. Birds sense approaching cold fronts and will often gorge themselves in anticipation of a storm. These pheasants all had bulging crops.

The third reason is that the field was very weedy. All corn-fields are not equal, which means that the better ones, whether you hunt them unharvested or take the more sensible approach and wait until they are picked, are those that contain cover in addition to the corn itself.

Actually, the birds didn't have many options. There was little CRP ground available to them that season. And from the actions of the pheasants we found along brushy creeks and in draws, it was obvious that those areas had been hunted hard. But the recently harvested cornfield hadn't been hunted and the birds still felt secure there.

Of course corn isn't a pheasant's only food, though it's certainly high on the list. The other major food item in my part of the country is soybeans. I've heard pheasant hunters say that ringnecks won't eat soybeans, but I've cleaned plenty of birds whose crops were stuffed with them. The difference is that you can't hunt soybean fields. Farmers normally harvest them before they combine corn, which means that the fields are usually bare by the time opening day rolls around. And when I say bare, I mean there won't be any cover at all after a combine has been through a soybean field.

If you do find a field that's unharvested when the season opens, do not try to hunt in it if you want to remain on friendly terms with the farmer. You and your dog will knock the pods off the plants, costing the farmer money. But hunting the edges of harvested soybean fields can be quite productive.

Conservation Reserve Program buffer strips consist of hundred-foot-wide borders along streams. They provide excellent cover for pheasants.

There are always waste beans left for the pheasants to glean. Of the two crops, however, the birds seem to prefer corn by a hefty margin.

Grain sorghum is another excellent pheasant food and is often planted in food plots on areas where the landowner (or state game commission, if it's public ground) is trying to attract wildlife. You won't see sorghum in vast quantities like you will corn or soybeans, but it's worth hunting wherever you find it.

Sunflowers are a popular crop in states like South Dakota and Kansas. I've found birds in close proximity to sunflowers in South Dakota. Although I can't recall finding the seeds in their crops, I'm sure they eat them.

Pheasants do eat weed seeds and can survive on them, but they much prefer agricultural crops. For one thing, it takes fewer kernels of corn to stuff a crop than it does the smaller weed seeds. In addition, food like corn and soybeans provide the higher nutrient and energy values the birds need to stay warm once the weather turns cold.

Pheasants and Waterways

Just as there are differences between CRP fields, the long, narrow areas I have referred to as strip cover also differ. I divide strip cover into three major subcategories: waterways, fencerows, and ditches.

Of these subcategories, waterways are my favorite. Fencerows are often too narrow and encourage pheasants to run, while road ditches force you to deal with passing traffic and the proximity of houses.

When it comes to waterways, I prefer those in the stream or small-creek size range; in other words, something not too wide or too deep. My dogs aren't trained to take hand signals, and if I drop a bird they don't mark on a creek's far bank, I may have to cross in order to get them in the area of the bird's fall. In those cases, I prefer a waterway narrow enough to jump or at least shallow enough to wade without getting too wet.

My absolute favorites are those streams with CRP buffer strips, or at least wide swaths of habitat along their banks. If a stream runs through or near picked corn or soybean fields, I can be fairly confident that birds will use its banks for cover.

A steep slope with several feet of drop to the waterline and cover all the way down its banks affords good winter habitat for late-season birds. Even if you hunt these areas early in the year, it is still a good idea to encourage your dog to drop over the edge to check things out. Where there is a relatively wide strip of cover above a sloping bank, one has a tendency to work the top and ignore what lies over the edge.

On a hunt in western Iowa several years ago, my friend Jim Cole and I were working a fenceline along a small creek with banks that dropped off abruptly. In a spot where the bank had eroded almost to the point of collapsing the fence, Heidi stuck her head through the wire and pointed.

I walked over behind her and looked down the weed-covered bank. I signaled Jim to join me.

"No way can I get down to flush the bird," I said. "Get ready and I'll kick some dirt over the edge." I sent a few clods rolling down the bank, bringing the rooster cackling out of his hiding place. The clever bird stayed below the top of the bank after he flushed, and although Jim and I both rocked him with our first barrels, it took my second shot to finish him off.

"I'll bet you anything that's an old rooster," I told Jim. When Heidi retrieved him, the bird's long, black spurs and streaming tailfeathers proved me right.

The English River in Poweshiek County, Iowa, is undoubtedly one of the more productive streams I have hunted. It is also fairly difficult for a lone hunter to work, even with a decent dog. A small stream, which hardly deserves the title of river in the stretches I've hunted, the English has steep banks that drop a good twenty feet from the fields above.

The problem with the English River, I discovered the first time I hunted it, was that most of the good habitat was below the top of the bank. There was only a narrow strip of cover adjacent to the farmed field above. Much of that, however, was choked with heavy brush and small trees. I convinced Heidi to drop over the edge and hunt the bank. The cover was too thick for me to work right above her, so I walked the field edge, out of sight of the dog. I listened carefully for any change in the music of her bell.

A white-tailed deer bounded up the bank on my side and out across the field about five yards in front of me. That temporary distraction caused me to lose track of Heidi, and the next thing I knew I couldn't hear her bell.

Picking a break in the thick cover, I shoved my way through to the top of the bank. All was in shadow below, and had it not been for Heidi's white tail-tip and blaze orange collar, I doubt that I would have been able to spot her dark form on point.

"Come on Heidi," I said. "That's where the deer was bedded down."

I'd just turned my back when I heard the distinctive sound of pheasant wings. I swung around and took a snap shot at a bird exiting downstream. Under the best of circumstances, I'm not good at shooting down on birds, and this was not the best of circumstances.

We hit a line fence and walked picked corn back to a nearby road. Disappointed but undaunted by the lack of birds on the river's north side, I decided the south bank was still worth a try. We worked the road's ditch down to the landowner's south-line fence a couple of hundred yards beyond the river. My plan was to follow the fence to the end of the field, work north to the river, then hunt back along the south bank.

Neither the road ditch nor the fencerow produced any

birds. However, the south bank was another story. Except in a couple of spots, it was open enough for me walk on top and look down on the dog. That gave me advance warning on the first bird, which didn't wait for Heidi to point. He bounced in the picked corn on our side of the stream, and I walked out to pick him up.

Bird number two came over a nice point. This one flushed while I was debating whether to chuck corncobs or to clamber down the bank. He was also an easy retrieve.

As I approached a thick patch of thorn bushes that were going to force me to detour into the field and out of sight of Heidi, she got very birdy. The rooster flushed from the heavy cover and I dropped him on the second shot, thankful that grouse hunting had taught me how to shoot through branches.

This bird dropped smack in the middle of the English River. Heidi was in her first season of hunting and had never made a water retrieve, so I was happy when she waded into the stream and picked up the soggy bird. Unfortunately, my happiness was premature—she decided that she did not like the taste of wet feathers and dropped the bird where she'd found him. No amount of coaxing or scolding could make her change her mind. I finally slithered down the bank and waded out, lucky that the temperature was above forty degrees and the water was only calf deep.

One of the secondary advantages of hunting creek-bank cover is that you can often pin the birds between you and the water. Although pheasants can swim, they'll rarely do so if they have options like sitting tight, running, or flushing. Experience has taught me that when faced with a stream more than about five feet wide, a pheasant will often stay put, typically down over the lip of the bank where two-legged hunters can't go and four-legged ones don't often go.

One problem my dogs and I had in 1988—one of the driest years I've experienced—was that the "bank strategy" didn't work in most places. Streams normally too wide to jump and too deep to wade didn't even have muddy bottoms.

Opening day should have tipped me off about things to come. Working the banks of what was usually a twenty-foot-wide, waist-deep creek, Heidi was clearly on a runner. When she locked up at the top of the bank, I felt certain I had the bird—there was virtually no cover on the other side of the creek.

Heidi seemed almost as stunned as I was when I walked by her and didn't flush anything. Then she took off down the creek bed in hot pursuit, raising dust as her feet hit the dirt. The bird turned out to be a youngster; had he not been, I'm sure he wouldn't have tried to sit it out in a little clump of weeds on the far bank.

That year, it didn't take the birds long to figure out that dry streams were perfect places to hunker down and run like hell. On some of the farms I hunted, the tracks in the dusty bottoms of the stream beds looked like herds of pheasants had been using them as highways.

Pheasants and Public Waterfowl Areas

In Chapter Two, I explained that public areas can be more productive than the average hunter would expect. They often consist of large blocks of heavy cover and can hold surprising numbers of birds. Let's consider one type of public hunting area in a bit more detail.

I've had some of my best hunting on public areas established with waterfowl in mind. Other hard-core pheasant hunters I know have had the same experience. Although there are other cover types in which I prefer to hunt, I have had excellent results working marshes, especially toward the end of the season. In fact, my final birds of at least five seasons came from public marshes. When you consider how much more time I spend on private land, you can see the value of these areas for late-season birds.

Duck marshes don't get a lot of pressure early because pheasant hunters correctly assume that the waterfowler's shooting and activity won't make for the best upland hunting situation. But in many places, waterfowl season closes well before pheasant season. By then most pheasant hunters have given up, and those who do work the marshes don't have a lot of competition.

One thing you must remember when going after marsh-dwelling pheasants is that most of these areas require nontoxic shot. That is the law on all federal Waterfowl Production Areas. The requirement on state-owned wetlands will vary from state to state.

The habitat on most public waterfowl areas will be denser than what you are likely to encounter on private land. Marsh ground is no prize to walk before it freezes, and even after ice-up it offers much trickier footing than traditional upland cover. It will wear you out in a hurry if you're not in shape, especially when it's cold and you are wrapped in several layers of clothing. But that is one reason why marshes are such good late-season cover. The birds are off the beaten path where many hunters lack either the capacity or the desire to go.

Public wetland areas, like big CRP fields, require a good

dog. Although my shorthairs can hunt this cover relatively well, it is better suited to flushing dogs, and particularly to the retrieving breeds.

Perhaps a good way to end this chapter on "Where to Hunt Pheasants" is by referring to the Pheasants Forever slogan, "Think Habitat." Habitat, or lack thereof, will make or break a bird population. Your selection of productive habitat, including its match to you, your hunting partners, and your dog's capabilities, will make or break the success of your hunt.

SEVEN

Pheasant-Hunting Tactics

I am a bit of a heretic on the subject of pheasant-hunting tactics, just as I am on the importance of weather. Both, in my opinion, are overemphasized.

Considering that I've discussed the use of various tactical maneuvers in preceding chapters, you may think it odd that I should now downplay the importance of the subject. However, most of the tactics I have described—driving standing corn and sneaking roadside ringnecks in particular—are maneuvers that I seldom use these days. My notebooks tell me that I bag at least 90 percent of my birds simply by turning one of my dogs loose and tagging along. If you have a good pair of legs, a good dog, and good cover to hunt, you will put birds in the bag without having to resort to clever maneuvers.

Tactics or Common Sense?

Much of what passes for pheasant-hunting tactics is, in my opinion, nothing more than common sense. You don't need a background in wildlife biology or animal behavior to hunt pheasants successfully. I am convinced that hunters who devise elaborate schemes to corner pheasants would bag more

189

Following a good dog in decent cover is often the best pheasant-hunting tactic.

birds if they spent less time scheming and more time walking.

Nevertheless, there are instances where planning can increase one's odds of getting a good shot at a rooster. Before we take a look at some of those situations, we need to consider what "tactics" are designed to accomplish.

You don't read much about tactics for hunting ruffed grouse, woodcock, or quail. In the case of grouse and woodcock, once you've located birds, the major problem is positioning yourself for a shot when you get a flush. Even when birds are pointed, the cover is often so thick that either you can't see the departing bird, or you and your gun are so tangled in the cover that you can't shoot. With forest-dwelling grouse and woodcock, there isn't much tactical planning that can be done.

Quail hunting may be even less tactical. In its classic form, it boils down to cutting dogs loose and following them. Once a covey is pointed, you can maneuver for good shots, as you do with grouse and woodcock. However, quail are usually in relatively open habitat, at least when compared to woodcock, and don't present the same difficulties. Trying to get between quail and the nearest escape cover is a tactic that is sometimes employed, though almost always unsuccessfully. Your presence on bobwhites' flight paths does nothing to discourage the birds, and little brown-bombs buzzing past your head are much harder to hit than when they are flying away from you.

Whoever invented pheasant tactics recognized a basic difference between pheasants and the birds mentioned above. When it comes to the desired means of escape, a pheasant would rather use its legs than its wings.

The ringneck's propensity to run lies at the heart of just

about every tactic I'm aware of. The problem, however, is that the birds can also fly. And in most types of their preferred cover they can simply sit tight and hide.

Driving standing corn, as I described in Chapter One, was almost certainly the first pheasant-hunting maneuver to come into widespread use. To review briefly, the successful ingredients for one of these operations includes the right amount of standing corn, the right number of hunters to drive the field and to block the end, and a goodly number of uneducated pheasants inhabiting the cornfield. Dogs are not a requirement and should not participate unless they are under the total control of their handler. The tactical objective is to make the pheasants run, but neither too far nor too fast. If this happens, they may scoot out the sides of the field beyond the range of the drivers but before they reach the blockers.

You don't see hunters driving standing corn much these days. Either there isn't any corn, or there is too much of it and too few people to mount a drive. Fields tend to be much larger these days than they were forty years ago.

That is not to say that the block-and-drive method will not work in other circumstances. Indeed it will, and it is probably the one tactic that every pheasant hunter needs to be aware of, whether or not he employs it very often.

But while driving and blocking can work in other situations, it is tailor-made for standing corn. Because of the way corn is planted, the fields are perfect for the maneuver— pheasants have nice lanes to run in, like track stars at the Olympics.

Blocking also works well in narrow cover, where the pheasant's options are limited. My notebooks remind me of one instance where it worked very well and provided the blocker with a story he's probably told many times since.

Jerry Fagle and I were pushing a narrow draw, about twenty yards across at its widest, through a combined soybean field. The cover in the draw was not heavy, allowing us to walk on either side while my pointer Jake made sure we didn't miss any birds.

It was deer season in Iowa and the blocker at the end of the draw, a friend of Jerry's, hadn't yet bagged a buck. Consequently, the blocker, who was shooting a 12-gauge pump, had a load of No. 6 shot in the chamber backed with slugs in the magazine. The idea was that he'd use the shot load on pheasants, or shuck it and cut loose with the slugs if he had a chance at a deer.

It was obvious from Jake's actions that we were moving birds, and it was equally obvious that they weren't likely to hold in the thin cover. As we approached within hailing distance of the blocker, I yelled at him to be ready.

Well before Jerry and I were within shooting range of where the draw dead-ended in bare ground, a rooster burst out and flew straight at the blocker. He made a nice passing shot.

Then a second bird flushed his way. Forgetting he had slugs behind the first load of shot, he cut loose again, dropping the second bird even harder than the first. That second bird, cleanly hit in the air with a slug, was missing the bottom third of its breast.

Because I've hunted with my own dogs for so many years, I've seldom had the opportunity to act as a blocker. I can't really say that I'm sorry because in spite of exceptions like the one I just mentioned, in my experience the drivers tend to get more shooting. They certainly get most of the chances at roosters that realize they're cornered and decide to sit tight. When I'm a driver, birds that hold usually result in points by my dogs and relatively easy shots.

On my first pheasant-hunting trip to South Dakota, in 1979, I was dogless. Well, not exactly dogless, but I knew that I'd be hunting with friends who had "good dogs," so I left my hawk-wild Irish setter at home. My familiar Sauer 16-gauge side-by-side was in the shop, which disturbed me much more than Nick the setter's absence. Just for the trip, I'd purchased a new Browning BSS—a straight-gripped, 20-gauge double, choked Improved Cylinder and Modified. I'd shot it well at woodcock, and although the Iowa pheasant season wasn't open yet, I felt ready for South Dakota ringnecks.

On that trip, because I was without a dog, I found myself in the unfamiliar position of blocker fairly often. On the first couple of drives, my friends were pushing through shelter-belts and the birds were coming out over the treetops. I fired several shots without result and began to blame the gun for my woes. In retrospect, I simply wasn't prepared to deal with shots the likes of which I had never seen before. The Sauer's longer barrels and heavier shot charge might have helped, but mainly I was out of my league with the South Dakota equivalent of British driven shooting.

Hunkered down behind a weedy fenceline, blocking for another drive, I was determined to request a chance to do some walking in the next field. That desire was reinforced by the number of shots I heard fired as the drivers approached.

Then I glanced to my left and saw a cock pheasant slinking under the barbed wire several fence posts down. I stood up. He took wing, and that Browning 20 gauge worked just fine on a shot that was familiar to me.

A variation of the block-and-drive method can be used in cooperation with a farmer. Often, when the last rows of corn are combined, a surprising number of birds will flush together. They do indeed love standing corn, and after they've been living in it and eating it for several weeks, they are reluctant to leave the security it offers them.

I hunted the 1973 opener with my father, brother, and nephew. My father had arranged for permission several weeks in advance and called ahead the night before to double-check. Fine, said the farmer, and he and Dad agreed that we would start our hunt the next morning in a specified field.

We were dealing with about eighty acres of corn, all but ten acres of which were picked. There were some narrow strips of corn left standing near the road, where we bagged a couple of birds during the first half-hour.

The end of the field farthest from the road contained the bulk of the standing corn. When the farmer showed up with his combine, we'd already hunted the narrow strips, and were making passes back and forth through the picked corn, gradually working toward the ten-acre plot of standing corn.

Here, were one to analyze our tactics, we were probably making an error. Novices might think that pheasants cannot run unseen in picked corn—and in so believing, they would be making an understandable but serious mistake. A rooster pheasant is an imposing bird when standing tall and stretching his neck. But when he runs, it is often in a crouch with his back not more than six inches from the ground.

In all probability, what we were doing by walking the picked corn was pushing birds into the remaining block of standing corn, which was too big for four of us to handle. Also, I was working Deke, my Moroccan Brittany, who had a low tolerance for birds running down rows of standing corn.

The farmer finished the narrow strips first, and we happened to complete one of our passes through the picked corn as he came up the fenceline, heading for the big plot of corn at the far end of the field. We showed him the birds we'd collected and then, typical of friendly Iowa landowners, he made a helpful suggestion.

"Keep an eye on me over there as I finish picking," he said, gesturing toward the standing corn. "Come join me when I'm ready to make my last couple of passes. Just walk beside the combine, and I'll bet you'll get some shooting."

Some farmers carry shotguns in the cabs of their combines, to put a rooster or two in the freezer. This one didn't, and as a result we added a couple of birds to our game bags.

Another farmer, whose land I hunted until he retired, made me a similar offer. I had arrived at his place early one afternoon as he was finishing the corn in a forty-acre field bounded on one side by a creek and on the other by a gravel road.

He suggested that I station myself in the ditch across the road from his field, directly in line with the last strip of standing corn. As has often been the case in my sporadic career as a blocker, the results were nil.

He pulled his combine out onto the road. "Can't understand where those birds all went," he said. "I picked half that field today and I saw at least a dozen of them running around when I first started. Didn't see a one flush."

197

I sized up the situation. "Maybe I'll try down along the creek," I said.

Jake and I headed into the wide, brushy strip of cover running along one side of the field and ending at the creek. About halfway down the strip, a rooster tried to escape out the far side of the fence. One in the bag. Several others, however, flushed out the end and across the creek before I was in range.

We turned and started working along the creek. There wasn't a lot of cover between the end of the corn rows and the bank, which descended abruptly some fifteen feet to the water below.

Jake's actions began to give me the idea that some of the birds had dropped over the edge. I was about to encourage him to hunt down the bank when two roosters flushed. Too eager for a double, I only feathered one of them with my first shot. But my second barrel sent him tumbling into the creek.

The birds in that field hadn't disappeared into thin air after all. Even though the last patch of standing corn had been surrounded by picked grain, the pheasants had managed to slink into the adjacent cover without the farmer spotting them, even from his vantage point in the combine high above the ground. In the end, I was much happier that he'd pushed them where I could hunt them with my dog than if he'd flushed them to me out on the road.

The Importance of Stealth

As a season wears on, pheasant behavior changes. The birds become increasingly wary of hunters through repeated encounters with guns and dogs. They are also likely to bunch up in thicker cover as much of their early-fall habitat is eliminated by normal farming activities. Add a fair amount of snow and you end up with a lot of birds in relatively small areas.

The block-and-drive tactic can be used on pheasants bunched in thick cover, but the hunters have to execute the maneuver to perfection. All likely escape routes have to be covered, and you have to use the element of surprise. Broadcast your approach to a bunch of nervous pheasants and they are almost certain to vacate the cover before you are within range. In my opinion, groups of pheasants are always tougher to work because of the tendency for all of them to fly when one flushes. And when birds have been pushed into small parcels of cover, they get even harder to hunt.

A few years ago, a half-dozen of us learned this lesson the hard way on a December hunt in northern Iowa. We had been hunting for most of the day without much luck. The snow was old and crusted, and although we were moving birds, they were flushing beyond gun range.

We decided it was time to use tactics to hunt an overgrown pasture with a creek running up the middle, surrounded by good cover. We chose a variation of the block and drive—a pincers maneuver. Three of us, myself included, would drop off at one end of the cover. We would approach the hoped-for pheasant sanctuary along a fenceline, across a quarter-mile of bare ground. The other three would drive to where a bridge crossed the creek, wait until we had crossed the open ground, then start toward us.

The problem was that the other three did not recognize the need for stealth. My group about halfway across the field when we saw their station wagon stop next to the bridge.

"I've got a bad feeling about this," I said quietly to my two partners. "I hope they wait to get out of the car until we're closer."

My mental telepathy didn't work. The first slam of the car door was enough to trigger a chain-reaction flush, and my group was still a long ways from being in position. I did the pheasant hunter's version of the hundred-yard dash and got there in time to take the last rooster as he rocketed over my head. But about fifty other birds, including a dozen roosters, had preceded him and flew straight down the cover, precisely where we would have been in couple of minutes.

The other three, chagrined at their mistake when we met in the middle of the now-birdless cover, told us that they hadn't intended to start hunting before we were in place; they were going to get out, load their guns, and wait. Obviously we should have emphasized the need for stealth in their part of the maneuver.

Putting a vehicle at one end of a strip of cover will sometimes keep birds from flushing. However, if hunters get out of the vehicle within a stone's throw of the cover, the result may be birds departing before the guns are even out of their cases. If blockers are in a vehicle, they should park it at least a hundred yards from where they intend to take up position. Even at that distance, they should avoid slamming doors and making noise getting into place.

There are secondary benefits to blocking, even when it does not prove effective in trapping birds. One advantage is that it can save a lot of unproductive walking. If you are working a narrow strip of cover in the middle of otherwise open ground, sending one hunter with a vehicle to the far end will spare you the effort of retracing your steps.

Working both sides of a fencerow may produce a rooster. It's an even more effective tactic if there's a blocker on the far end.

The maneuver can also be used to make things easier on hunters who, for whatever reason, can't walk for a full day. Allowing them the respite afforded by blocking may be the only way they can keep up with the rest of the group.

Iowa topography lends itself to other kinds of blocking or pincers maneuvers in addition to the classic standing-corn drive. For the most part, when viewed from the air the state looks like a huge checkerboard neatly laid out in square miles with gravel roads forming the perimeter of each section. This results in numerous narrow strips of cover a mile long—waterways, fencerows, and road ditches, for example.

These can be worked effectively by two or three hunters with a vehicle. If such covers are narrow enough, they are

This hunter and his dog have trapped a bird against a dirt road, and it has nowhere to go but up.

as well designed for dogless hunters as it is possible to find.

One hunter—two if the cover is wide enough—starts at one end. The other hunter takes the vehicle to the far side of the section and either blocks at that point or works back toward his approaching companion. This is an excellent maneuver, particularly in narrow strips. The birds will often run, but by putting someone at the far end you have a better chance of cornering them.

Tactics for the Solo Hunter

I spend a good deal of time hunting alone, so I don't have many opportunities to work clever maneuvers. However, I have found one tactic that does put an occasional extra bird in the bag. For lack of a better name, I call it "reverse logic."

Conventional wisdom has it that you should work cover in such a way that you cut off the birds' opportunities to run. The draw that comes to an end in the middle of an open field is one example. Another is the waterway that has good cover on one farmer's ground, but has been cultivated right up to its banks on the adjacent farm. You push to where the cover ends, and somewhere near that end at least one or two roosters should sit tight.

That approach works well early in the season. Eventually, however, the birds become accustomed to hunters coming after them from the same direction. Try going against conventional wisdom by pushing back into the cover. Logic may tell you that you are working the birds so they can run on you, but occasionally the novelty of the approach seems to confuse them.

Using this tactic in Iowa usually means an approach along a barren fencerow or across an open field to reach your destination, then pushing the cover out to a road ditch. Get ready when you hit the ditch. Although ditches often have good cover and the birds could turn left or right and keep running, they frequently elect to sit tight.

Hunters with dogs are often well advised to forget about tactics entirely. The obvious approach as you see it may not be the best way to use your dog to its greatest advantage. I always try to hunt good-looking cover into the wind, regardless of whether this seems logical from the standpoint of human tactics.

Using the wind properly is especially important in dry conditions, when scenting is tough. Give your dog every opportunity to use his nose most effectively.

Hunting into the wind can be useful even for the dogless

hunter. Wind makes birds jumpy, and it will carry the sounds of even a stealthy, lone hunter a surprising distance—especially so to the sharp ears of a pheasant. Using the wind to conceal your approach may allow you to surprise the same birds that would never let you get within range if you came at them with the wind behind you.

Working slowly and thoroughly in heavy cover, with or without a dog, is also preferable to charging through the brush at breakneck speed. In thick stuff, even a good dog needs to take its time. If the birds are not moving much, there are a lot of potential hiding spots that must be checked. On the other hand, if you are into birds that are moving, the dog may lock onto one, trail it, and miss others. Either way, by moving too fast, you and your dog may miss birds that are holding tight.

How many times have you almost stepped on a bird when your dog was hunting elsewhere? This is often not the dog's fault. Quail hang out in nice, tight coveys. Grouse are found scattered for the most part. If you are into a woodcock flight, you can push a lot of birds out of a small area, but they don't usually move around that much, leaving confusing scent trails for your dog.

Pheasants, on the other hand, can be found in large but loosely knit bunches. Just try to sort out tracks, even in fresh snow, in a piece of cover inhabited by plenty of birds. This is what your dog is trying to do with scent, and why he may appear to miss birds. If you do flush a bird, you've probably found one that your dog hasn't gotten around to yet. Give him the time he needs to work the cover.

But don't overdo the "slow and cautious" approach, especially if you have an experienced dog. My notebooks remind me of an opening-day hunt with a party that included one hunter I didn't know. It became clear that he knew little about reading dogs, in particular my shorthair Heidi, who had seen far more pheasants than he had.

We were working a waterway with heavy cover along its banks, at what I thought was a reasonable pace. It was a dark, cold morning and my guess that the birds had yet to start moving around was reinforced by the fact that Heidi was not picking up scent. The veteran shorthair was sweeping back and forth through the cover, giving it a thorough going-over.

But the skeptical hunter thought our pace was too fast, though we had yet to flush a bird the dog had missed. The other members of the party knew Heidi and trusted her. But the skeptic insisted, so we let him tag along behind us, which would have made me nervous had I thought he was actually going to find bypassed birds.

By the time we reached the far end of the waterway, the three of us who stuck with the dog had collected a rooster apiece. Tail-end Charlie hadn't even flushed a hen. Heidi made another convert; the man stuck with the rest of us—and kept a particularly close eye on the dog—for the rest of the hunt.

Rushing through cover behind a dog may be justified if the cover is relatively thin and if it is apparent that the birds are running. In such a situation, you are probably better off hustling after your dog and hoping that you get close enough for a shot.

I want to end this chapter on the same point that began it. Clever tactical maneuvers can be effective in certain situations, but most of the time following a good dog in good cover is the only tactic you really need to put birds in the bag.

EIGHT

Roosters I Have Known

Although more praise has been heaped upon ruffed grouse and bobwhite quail than pheasants, in my opinion ringnecks have greater individuality. You can make accurate generalizations about pheasants, but there are plenty of individual birds that don't fit the mold—birds that stand out clearly in my memory of four-plus decades of gunning pheasants.

There is one generalization, however, that every pheasant hunter knows to be true. Among our most popular gamebirds, the rooster pheasant is the one that, as the old saw goes, "takes a licking and keeps on ticking." I've seen birds hit three times and somehow manage to keep flying.

I've already described the phenomenon of pheasants that fly on after being hit, then suddenly die in mid-flight. Writer Phil Bourjaily was involved in an extreme case—the longest flight I've ever witnessed by a "dead but doesn't know it" bird.

Phil and I were finishing a hunt in Poweshiek County, Iowa, talking over the birds we got and the ones that got away, when I noticed that my shorthair Blitz was nowhere to be seen. When I whistled and got no response, I figured she was on point somewhere, though there weren't many options. We had pulled up a steep field-driveway and parked the truck in cut corn, not far from the fence bordering the road. Blitz wasn't visible anywhere along the fenceline, so I walked down the driveway to the gravel road below. From there I spotted her locked up in the road ditch, near the top of the bank, on the road side of the fence. I alerted Phil that he should get his gun and load up.

The bank Blitz had climbed would have been a steep scramble for me, so I walked back up the driveway and directed Phil to approach the shorthair from the field side of the fence. The rooster, caught between dog and approaching hunter, flushed obligingly. Phil swung on the bird and fired twice with no apparent effect. It was one of those "I could have sworn I hit the bird" situations. We watched the rooster sail across a CRP field on the other side of the road, then tumble from the sky—obviously dead just as he crested a hill in the field.

Without any visible mark to guide us and with the bird down on the far side of the hill, that was one we never found. But it must have flown a quarter-mile before dropping out of the sky.

True Doubles and Quick Limits

As I've stated, I have very few true doubles on pheasants to my credit. A true double, at least to "purists"—in this case I'll stick with their definition—involves shooting two birds that are in the air simultaneously. Although my notebooks mention a couple of occasions when I've missed chances at shooting a double, such opportunities are relatively rare. Because of a pheasant's ability to carry shot, hunters should be cautious about taking doubles. The problem is that most of us have trouble resisting such an opportunity, and instinct takes over before our brain considers such things as the quality of the shot, density of the cover, and location of the dog. All of these factors influence the success of retrieving a double, even when the gunner succeeds in knocking down both birds.

Some of my best chances for doubles presented themselves in situations where I couldn't take advantage of them. By way of an example, during one hunt my partner and I had both shot limits and were on our way out of the field when Heidi hit a nice point. The sky was a bright blue, a picture-perfect day. I asked my partner to walk in and flush the bird while I snapped some photos. Two roosters came up, one right after the other, in what would have been a ideal opportunity for a double. Unfortunately, I didn't even capture the birds on film.

There are days when you walk for miles without moving a single pheasant—the birds seem to have dropped off the map. Then there are the other hunts, when limits happen almost too quickly.

Two old friends of mine, Jim Cole and Doug Carpenter, had invited me to join them for a hunt near Denison in western Iowa. Never having hunted that area before but having heard good things about the bird population, I was eager to give it a try.

The first day of the hunt was cold and windy, and we struck out totally in the morning. Things did pick up a bit in the afternoon. I dropped two birds over Heidi's solid points along brushy creeks. We finished the day in a large CRP field where my pointer Rebel found several pheasants. Unfortunately, Jim and I missed one easy chance, and I wing-tipped a bird that escaped through a woven wire fence that cut off Rebel's pursuit. Finally, Doug dropped a rooster at the end of shooting hours.

The next morning our local guide, Vic Thomsen, took us along Paradise Creek. The name turned out to be appropriate. Doug was walking a high bank on one side of the creek while Vic, his twelve-year-old son Greg, and I worked the other side, which had most of the good cover.

In addition to the grassy-edged creek, there was also a nearby road ditch that was within gunshot of the creek in most places. The ditch produced a point by Heidi and a kill for Vic.

Then Doug hailed me from the other side. "There's some good cover on your bank," he called. "I think you'd better take Heidi through it."

When I got close enough to look over the creek bank, I saw what Doug meant. A small, sandy peninsula, choked with willows and brush, jutted out into the water.

Heidi no more than had her nose into the cover when two roosters flushed; one angled to the right while the other went to the left. Leaving the right-hand bird to Doug, I drew down on the second rooster, dropping him on the high bank across the creek, well in front of my partner.

Doug was still looking the other way at the right-hand bird, which had managed to escape him. I broke my gun, dropped in a fresh shell, and yelled, "You've got a dead bird down in front of you. Heidi's coming across the creek."

I took a step forward and another rooster flushed straight away from me. I dropped it on my side of the water. As I brought my gun down another bird came crashing out of the willows on a flight line similar to that of the first bird I'd killed. My left barrel took this one, which didn't quite clear the high bank on the far side. It rolled down the embankment, coming to rest about halfway between the top of the bank and the creek.

That entire sequence—three birds dead—took less than thirty seconds. It is by far the fastest I have ever killed a limit.

Heidi, bringing back my first bird from the creek's far side, nearly stepped on the third dead rooster as she came down the bank. Looking a bit bewildered, she paused as if trying to figure out how to get two of them in her mouth, then decided it couldn't be done and brought me the one she already had.

Twelve-year-old Greg walked over to where I was standing, his eyes the size of half-dollars, and said, "You sure were right about creeks being good spots!" He'd just read an article I'd written about the benefits of hunting pheasant along waterways.

Unusual Roosters

Most pheasant hunters know that the birds can be very hard or very easy to hunt, while sportsmen with enough rooster-chasing under their belts also realize that ringnecks can be just plain strange from time to time.

My first really unusual experience with a pheasant goes back to the days before I carried a gun, probably almost fifty years ago. I was sitting in my family's 1948 Dodge waiting for my father to come back from a brief "tromp" along a road ditch. As he approached the car, I noticed that he had a rooster in hand. Curious because I hadn't heard a shot, I asked what had happened.

"Somebody must have crippled this bird," he replied. "I stepped on it in the weeds, but it couldn't fly. I just picked it up and banged its head on a fence post."

When we reached home, both of us were surprised to find the bird sitting up and giving us the the evil eye from a corner of the car's trunk. Dad took the bird down to the basement, where we cleaned our game. Perhaps through shock or the strangeness of the surroundings, the bird seemed to have no fear of people. The big rooster, apparently only wing-broken, strutted around and checked everything out, oblivious to our presence.

Cleaning a bird that was already dead was one thing. Killing one that was strolling innocently around the basement was another. I suggested to Dad that we keep it as a pet, but he explained to me that the game warden would frown on such a thing. Having become acquainted with that bird, I had to leave the scene before Dad dispatched him.

My second close encounter with an overly healthy pheasant took place about the time I finished high school. A school chum and I were bird hunting in deep snow. As we walked along looking for tracks (we were hunting dogless), I noticed a set of rooster tailfeathers protruding from the snow right between my feet. There were no tracks around, and I made the logical assumption that someone had killed a bird on that spot days earlier.

"Look at this," I called to my friend, then reached down to pick up the feathers. "Someone got a . . ."

I never finished the sentence. Just as I grabbed the feathers, a very lively rooster, firmly attached to the other end of the tail, flushed and showered me with snow. Both of us shot and missed. All I had to show for it were the bird's two longest feathers, which he'd left in my hand in his haste to depart. Either he'd flown directly into the snow and stayed there, or freshly fallen snow had covered his tracks and everything else except his tail. In either case, he was safe but sporting less magnificent plumage.

As a result of that experience, the second time a pheasant's tail gave away its presence I was more cautious. My brother Errol, my nephew Randy, and I were returning home from a hunt. As we drove along the highway, we spotted a group of hunters some distance from us in a field adjacent to the road.

Several birds flushed in front of them. I watched as one bird, clearly hit, sailed across the road and landed in the ditch on the opposite side.

"Stop the car!" I told my brother abruptly, then explained to him what had happened. By this time we were some distance beyond the spot where the rooster had gone down. Errol made a U-turn and headed back down the road.

I was sure that I had the bird marked within twenty or thirty yards one way or the other. I suggested that we take our guns, in case the rooster was able to fly or run, and search the area. The hunters across the road from us apparently hadn't seen it come down and had headed in the opposite direction.

The ditch had several inches of light snow in it, so I figured that finding the bird would be a cinch. But after working down the ditch far beyond where I'd marked him, then back over this area again, we hadn't seen a track. It was near zero and the wind was blowing hard. Both Randy and Errol headed to the car.

"I'm going to make one more try," I said. "That bird can't have disappeared."

This time, looking hard for tracks, blood, or any other sign, I focused my efforts on the fence that separated the ditch from the adjacent field. The fenceline was where I thought the bird had landed and because it had clumps of weedy cover, that seemed the most logical place for the bird to hide.

About a half-dozen fence posts down the line from where I had started my search, I spotted two footprints, and what appeared to be a weed sticking from the snow. A closer look showed it to be tailfeathers.

My dilemma was that the feathers barely protruded through my side of the fence. The bird was just on the other side and the three-strand fence was high enough that I could-n't step over it. The last thing I wanted was to have the roost-er flush or run when I had one foot on the bottom strand of wire and the other suspended in space.

I tried kicking the fence, throwing snow on the bird, and shouting, "Hey, get out of there!" Nothing happened. I thought perhaps the bird had made it that far and died.

I knelt down gingerly, reaching for the tailfeathers with my left hand and keeping my gun as ready as I could in my right. When I gave the tailfeathers a pull, the rooster pulled the other way. Although he was unable to fly, both legs were quite healthy, and I took him on the ground as he raced across the snow.

Speaking of unusual birds and their tails, the longest feather I've ever collected measured over twenty-six inches and came from a big rooster that had no spurs. I could see spots on his legs where spurs belonged, but he didn't even have the "bumps" typical of juveniles. I have always wondered whether that bird never developed spurs or whether he broke them off fighting or through some type of accident. The latter

Tailfeather length is a good measure of a bird's age. This rooster is probably into his second season.

would seem a more likely possibility if only one of the two spurs had been missing.

Long, black spurs and a long tail usually go together and are a good indication that the bird is in at least his second season. My spurless bird was an exception to this rule. A rooster I shot on Christmas Eve in 1989, on a public hunting area along the Des Moines River, was an exception of a different sort. He sported the long, pointed spurs of a veteran, but his tail measured a mere twenty inches.

But top prize for the most unusual bird of my hunting career has nothing to do with its tail or spurs. I remember it so clearly because of the circumstances surrounding our encounter.

I was hunting near Anamosa in eastern Iowa with my friend Denny Conrad. My canine assistant at the time was Nick, the "Red Rocket," my legendary Irish setter, who had been behaving so badly that he didn't make the trip.

Hunting dogless, Denny and I were on opposite sides of a narrow creek. We were within gunshot of a fence that crossed the creek ahead of us when a rooster flushed about ten yards in front of me. As I raised my shotgun, the low-flying bird hit the top strand of the fence, somersaulted, and landed hard on its back in open pasture on the opposite side. I hustled up to the fence, where I saw the bird with its feet in the air, either dead or badly stunned.

Once again I was confronted with a fence too high to step over. I was trying to avoid being caught in an impossible situation if the bird flushed, so I decided that the best course was to frighten him into taking wing if he was able to do so.

"Come on, get up! Fly!" I yelled at the prostrate rooster,

which was lying only a few paces beyond the fence.

Finally, the rooster struggled to his feet, looked at me, and took a couple of wobbly steps in the opposite direction. He flapped his wings in an abortive takeoff attempt, briefly touched his landing gear to the ground again, then succeeded in getting airborne. I saluted the bird's departure with two misses.

Denny, who had heard me talking to the bird, then saw me miss, came over for an explanation. Initially, all I could do was shake my head in amazement. Then we both had a good laugh about how that bird had made a double escape—first from his collision with the fence, and second from my off-target shots.

Dave Prine and his chocolate Labrador Hoss provided an interesting experience for me on a hunt in Mahaska County, Iowa. Working some dense cover, Hoss dove into the weeds and came out with a rooster in his mouth.

"Dog got a cripple?" I called to Dave as he took the bird from Hoss.

"No, there's nothing wrong with this bird," said Dave, catapulting it into the air. I was stunned for a second but recovered quickly enough to drop the departing bird.

Dave, who shoots live pigeons from time to time, had a big grin on his face. "Bet I'm the only *columbaire* who's ever thrown a pheasant," he joked.

My notes from the 1989 season reveal a curious incident from a separate hunt along a creek in northern Iowa. The creek ran through a weedy field that, judging from the vegetation, was a marsh in wet years. However, 1989 was a dry year and there was no water anywhere except in the stream. The creek itself was too wide and too deep to cross, and was not yet frozen solid.

We'd just come through a patch of especially heavy cover with weeds about waist high. Heidi was definitely working birds, but she seemed confused, usually an indication that more than one bird was running. She circled in a patch of lighter cover, trying to pick up the trail.

Just then a rooster went out low to my extreme left. I folded the bird and hustled to the area of its fall, afraid it might have dropped into the denser cover on the far side of the creek.

When I got to the stream, I spotted the bird on the thin ice, just short of the far bank. It was lying on its side, motionless, with the wind ruffling its feathers. Heidi finally saw the rooster and I ordered her to retrieve. She stepped gingerly onto the ice and made it about halfway across before she broke through. She struggled for a half-minute or so, breaking ice each time she tried to pull herself up. I was ready to go in after her when she managed to extricate herself.

Heidi was not interested in testing the ice in another spot, nor was I going to try it. I decided to go down the creek on my side, cross the road bridge a quarter-mile farther on, then come back on the opposite side and pick up the bird.

About that time my "dead" bird came to life. He stood up, eying me suspiciously for several seconds. I was too close for a shot, so I turned to Heidi, hoping the sight of the cripple would trigger another attempt to cross the creek.

As I urged her to go get the bird, the pheasant hopped up into the weeds on the other side. I fired, which was all the encouragement Heidi needed. She scooted across the creek, ahead of the cracking ice, hot after the bird. He came racing out of the cover and back onto the ice about ten yards farther down, where I ended his gaudy career once and for all.

During the many years I've hunted ringnecks, I've seen crippled roosters kick, peck, beat their wings, and do everything else in their power to tangle with the dog that's been sent to fetch them—that is, when they are finally cornered. But their preferred tactics are either to hide (usually when their legs are broken) or to run if both legs are in working order. I've seen only one wounded pheasant actually attack a dog when it had a clear escape route.

This incident took place during the Iowa Governor's Pheasant Hunt on opening day of the 1995 season. After starting the morning with my ten-year-old veteran Heidi, I'd switched to her daughter Blitz—then in her second season—as we hunted a couple of small fields before lunch.

When it became apparent that most of the group were going to be a few minutes catching up with us, Blitz and I headed into a corner of a field that had received scant attention on our first pass. Sure enough, where two fences met, Blitz slammed into a hard point.

When the rooster flushed, I dropped him on the far side of the fence, in a bare pasture. Unfortunately, the fence was woven wire instead of standard barbed wire, meaning that a dog must go over it rather than between the strands. I'd put down my gun to give Blitz a boost when the bird took off running, down the fenceline. I grabbed for my gun to finish the rooster, but he stayed within two or three feet of the fence on his side, while Blitz was kept pace on her side. I couldn't shoot the bird for fear of hitting the dog, so I hustled along behind, waiting for the bird to turn away from the fence and give me a safe shot.

After bird and dog had raced for maybe one hundred and fifty yards, with me trailing behind, the pheasant stopped in his tracks. Instead of running into the bare pasture and offering me a shot, he spread his wings and charged the dog on the far side of the fence. This took Blitz by surprise, and she recoiled temporarily. But when the daring rooster tried the maneuver a second time, Blitz was ready. The bird got his head through the wire, at which point Blitz grabbed it and pulled him through the fence.

That gutsy rooster made up in courage what he lacked in brains.

Odd-Looking Birds

Just as you will occasionally encounter odd-acting birds, you will almost certainly run across odd-looking birds. The pheasant in America is such a hybrid that this should come as no surprise.

However, there is a more common reason that some birds don't look quite right. The fact that pheasant broods in the same area will hatch several weeks apart—and sometimes as much as two or three months apart—makes for big differences in appearance, especially early in the season.

On opening weekend several years ago, my friend Gene Kroupa shot the smallest rooster I have ever seen bagged. Only the red patches around the bird's eyes gave it away. Gene told me that if the bird hadn't flown past him at close range, he never would have known it was a cock.

The longer I hunt pheasants, the more convinced I am that some roosters make it through opening weekend because they can't be distinguished from hens. In 1989, my opening-day party accounted for two tailless roosters that might well have survived had it not been a bright, sunny day. A week later, Mike Carroll and I let a bird reach extreme range before we fired because, until he let out a juvenile half-cackle, we thought he was a hen.

My notebook and a photo remind me of a particularly odd-looking bird I shot several years ago. It was December, a time when even young roosters have full plumage and long tails, unless the latter have been shot off.

Four of us were hunting abreast through a wide strip of weeds leading to a picked cornfield, when a bird flushed from left to right in front of us. I was on the extreme right side of our line. Mike Carroll, to my immediate left, fired as the bird crossed in front of him. He pulled tailfeathers, and I finished the bird.

When I spotted Rebel coming in with the pheasant in her mouth, I started to berate Mike. The bird looked like a hen. I told him that I wouldn't have shot if he hadn't fired first.

"I'm sure that bird's a rooster," said Mike. All I could see were tan feathers, so I wasn't convinced. However, upon closer examination I discovered that Mike was right. The bird had a dark head, dark breast feathers, and a full pair of spurs. Wildlife biologists later told me that the bird was a fluke. Occasionally pheasants, similar to domestic chickens, produce individuals with characteristics of both sexes—like hen chickens that crow. But in all the years I've hunted, that's the only late-season, full-grown bird I've ever seen that looked more like a hen than a rooster.

It is amazing that roosters resemble one another as much as they do, when you consider all the strains of pheasants that

Undoubtedly the most unusual-looking pheasant the author has ever shot. The bird flew right by him, and it was only the red eye patch that told him for sure that it was a rooster.

have been imported into the U.S. I have seen several true albinos mounted, although I wonder if they were wild birds—some shooting preserves offer albino pheasants as a novelty. I have only encountered one in the wild, but I've spoken to other experienced hunters who say that they've also seen white pheasants.

Although I've never had a shot at an albino, I've killed a couple of other odd-looking roosters. The first came over Jake, my pointer. Unfortunately the bird didn't hit the ground dead and Jake, who had had too many roosters peck him, spur him, and wing-beat him in the face, got a bit rough. The dog didn't mangle the bird, but it was not a good specimen for the taxidermist.

This particular rooster looked relatively normal except for

its wings, which were white, and its head, which was white with black spots. I shot it near the town of Clarksville, Iowa, and there were no shooting preserves or game farms anywhere in the vicinity. Although that is not an area where I've hunted a lot, I did see the albino bird I mentioned a moment ago less than ten miles from there. Other people who hunt that area frequently tell me that it seems to have more than its share of odd-looking birds.

The second mostly white pheasant that I shot came from a farm that I had hunted for years. I was with my friend Joe Cornett when the bird flushed over Heidi's point, and if I hadn't seen the red eye patch, I wouldn't have known it was a rooster. I called for Joe to shoot, but he told me afterward that it was such an odd creature he couldn't pull the trigger. I did shoot and hit the bird hard, so it also was not a good candidate for mounting. But I do have a foot-long, white tailfeather (it must have been a bird of the year) to remind me.

There were no preserves anywhere near that farm and the landowner, who is an old friend, told me he'd never seen strangely colored birds on his place, nor had other hunters reported them.

Certainly by their actions as well as by their appearance, a few pheasants seem to stand out from among the many I encounter every season. To me that is just another of the many charms of the birds and the sport of hunting them.

NINE

A Mixed Bag

Here I'll cover topics that are of importance to pheasant hunters but that don't rate individual chapters and don't fit into other sections of this book.

Since we're going to talk about a "mixed-bag," multiple-species hunts seem like a good place to start.

Mixed-Bag Bird Hunts

Throughout much of their range, pheasants are found in close company with other upland birds. In fact, some hunters seek situations where they are going to be surprised by what materializes when they step in front of their pointing dog, or by what their retriever or spaniel flushes from the brush.

Most of my mixed-bag experience comes from pheasant and bobwhite quail combo-hunts. This kind of shooting used to be fairly common in parts of Iowa, Kansas, and Nebraska. Unfortunately, in recent years the quail population has declined significantly in Iowa and Nebraska, though Kansas birds have suffered a bit less.

Quail purists will shudder at the thought, but there are Midwestern hunters who do just fine gunning bobwhites in front of flushing dogs. It may not be classic hunting, but it produces results. My fellow Iowan Dave Prine claims that he actually prefers shooting quail in front of his Labs, though he bags several times as many pheasants in a normal season.

The main problem with a pheasant and quail mixed-bag shoot is choosing guns and ammunition. An open-choke 20 gauge (or even 28 gauge) shooting less than an ounce of No. 8 shot is fine for quail but too light for pheasants, while a tight choke and No. 6 shot is far from ideal for quail.

An ounce of No. 7 1/2 shot is a good compromise load, although it restricts your range on pheasants. If I'm in quail country, I'll load No. 7 1/2s in the right barrel and No. 6s in the left. If we bust a covey and go after the singles, I'll change to 7 1/2s in both barrels.

On one memorable occasion, Mike Carroll and I were loading up to hunt a piece of public land near Rathbun Reservoir in southern Iowa. From the road, I spotted a number of pheasants as they sailed into a grassy draw about a quarter-mile away. We both loaded No. 6s and went after the birds.

Deke, my Brittany, was doing the point-and-move maneuver typical of a dog working running pheasants. I was watching him intently, waiting for him to lock up, when I stepped into the middle of a covey of quail. With the impression only flushing quail can give, I thought that I must have disturbed a nest of giant, feathered hornets. Birds seemed to be buzzing out everywhere.

I tried to pick out a single but hit only air. Mike, never a slow man on the trigger, got off two quick shots with his 20-gauge double. The second shot resulted in a big puff of feathers. Deke broke off his search for pheasants to make the retrieve. The biggest piece of the bobwhite he could find was a wing. The heavy load of No. 6 shot from a full-choke barrel at under twenty yards literally blew that bird apart. Meanwhile, the pheasants were flushing to safety out of the draw's far end.

On another occasion, I was hunting solo with Jake on a southeastern Iowa farm where I knew that I was more likely to find pheasants than quail. We were working the edge of a strip of woods beside a picked soybean field. Without warning, Jake slammed on point at the edge of a dense patch of multiflora rose. That type of cover and Jake's lack of "birdy" warning before he locked up made me guess quail rather than pheasant. When the rooster flushed, I blew an easy chance with the first barrel, then recovered my composure and dumped him on the second shot.

I broke my shotgun, congratulated myself, and waited for Jake to retrieve the rooster from the soybean field where it had fallen. Instead, the dog stiffened into a point next to a tiny patch of foxtail—maybe two feet by ten feet—in the middle of otherwise bare ground. The rooster was on the far side of the foxtail, and I assumed that Jake was pointing dead.

I began to get suspicious when he refused to fetch at my command. I took a step forward and began to pluck the empty shells from the gun. As I did so, about fifteen quail rose in unison from the tiny patch. All I could do was stand with an unloaded gun and watch the birds depart. I had dropped the rooster, which flushed from perfect bobwhite habitat, about five yards from a covey hiding in a piece of cover so small that no one would have expected quail to be there.

A rooster flanked by a brace of gray (Hungarian) partridge—a common mixed bag.

Perhaps the motto of the mixed-bag hunt should be, expect the unexpected.

Fortunately for pheasant hunters, other birds often found in combination with pheasants present less of a guns-and-ammo problem. In places like Montana, the Dakotas, Nebraska, and to a lesser extent Iowa, Hungarian partridge, sharp-tailed grouse, and prairie chickens are often taken on mixed-bag hunts. However, the same gun and load you use for pheasants work well on those species.

Washington, Oregon, and Idaho offer a gamebird smorgasbord. Along with pheasants, it's possible to bag valley and mountain quail, ruffed and blue grouse, and chukar on the same hunt. But these birds are not usually found in the same habitat as pheasants, whereas prairie grouse and bobwhites often are. So you're less likely to be surprised by their appearance—most of the time.

Of course there are mixed-bag problems for which solutions are not readily apparent. Some years ago on a late-October woodcock hunt along the Missouri River in western Iowa, I found pheasants and timberdoodles living in close proximity. The woodcock hung out in thick willows where not much grass had grown. The roosters hid toward the edge of the cover, where the trees were thinly spaced and the grass thicker. I even found a covey of bobwhites along the edge of a small cornfield in the same area.

Although Jake nearly abandoned me because I didn't shoot the pheasants he pointed—the pheasant opener was still a week away—I had no problem with selection of gun and load. Had I returned the following weekend, and had woodcock still been in residence, I'm not sure how I would have handled that combination.

I know of one public hunting area in Iowa where you used to be able to shoot grouse, woodcock, pheasants, and quail. You can still find the first three birds, but the place is on the northern fringe of quail range and I haven't seen a covey there in years. But just a couple of seasons ago, Blitz got birdy along an edge where I've shot plenty of woodcock over the seasons. I started to suspect, however, that we weren't dealing with a timberdoodle when she pointed her nose at a clump of thick grass. When the half-grown rooster flushed, I saluted his luck that pheasant season hadn't yet opened.

My longtime partner Mike Carroll and I once collected a pair of roosters and a brace of ruffed grouse from the same cover. Pheasant loads, though a bit heavy, will work for grouse. But if you're expecting a ruff and a hen pheasant flushes instead, there is more than a little potential for a case of mistaken identity.

What to Wear—Clothing and Footgear

These days, pheasant hunters are giving more thought to what they wear afield. As long as fashion equates to practicality—clothing that will keep me dry, either warm or cool enough, and won't hinder my shooting—I'm all for it.

It's a far cry, however, from what my father wore. His pheasant-hunting "uniform" usually consisted of bib overalls over a flannel shirt, supplemented in cold weather by a hip-length denim jacket known among farmers as a "chore coat." Dad spent part of his youth on a farm, and he knew the utility of typical farmer garb. He also knew that he stood a better chance of getting permission to hunt private land if he didn't look like a city slicker. This was before blaze orange, so he wasn't any harder to see in his outfit than other contemporary hunters. Perhaps easier, because the popular color of hunting coats and vests back then was brown, which blended better with corn, weeds, and dead grass than did blue denim. Other than the lack of a game bag in which to carry roosters, his choice of clothing was practical.

But let's look at the functional purpose of modern clothing—namely, keeping you comfortable and not hindering your shooting—by starting from the bottom and getting dressed for a hunt.

Other than a shotgun and ammunition, boots are the most critical items in a hunter's gear box. A friend of mine nearly ruined a South Dakota pheasant hunt—not to mention his feet—by using the hunt to break in a new pair of boots that didn't fit quite right. If you're going to buy new boots, do so well before the season, make sure they fit properly, and break them in thoroughly.

I used to do much of my pheasant hunting in L. L. Bean boots, the much-copied old standby with rubber bottoms and leather tops. Although they are not perfect for any specific circumstances, Bean boots are still a pretty good choice because they work reasonably well in just about all conditions you'll encounter in ringneck country. It has to be soaking wet, extremely cold, or very hot before L. L. Bean boots are a poor choice. However, I have heard the criticism that they are not the best selection for people who need more foot and ankle support. But if they aren't the best first choice, they are nearly always a very good second choice. L. L. Bean boots are inexpensive as hunting footwear goes, and having them along as spares is a good idea.

My preference these days runs to leather or combination leather-cordura boots with light (200 gram) Thinsulate insulation and a Gore-Tex liner. They are warmer than uninsulated Bean boots, yet my feet get no hotter in warm weather. And they are generally waterproof.

A word here about the reality of "waterproof." Just being able to wade rapidly across a stream without getting your feet wet is not a true test of your boot's watertightness. Try walking for several hours in wet grass or snow. If your feet stay dry under those conditions, then your boots are truly waterproof. Typically, new Gore-Tex boots will keep you dry, but after extensive wear you'll find that they offer increasingly less protection if you're in wet cover for hours.

The only completely waterproof boots I've found, at least over the long haul, are made of rubber. You can spend hundreds of dollars on top-of-the-line rubber boots, and what you get is a special lining that keeps your feet from getting as wet as they do in cheaper versions. Remember, with rubber boots moisture is produced on the inside by your feet, and without a quality boot lining they will get wet and quite cold.

That said, I don't spend a lot of money on rubber boots. The reason is that I do virtually all my pheasant hunting in farm country, which is also barbed-wire fence country. Sooner or later, barbed wire or something else with a sharp edge or point will punch a hole in rubber boots, no matter how much you paid for them. It's true that you can patch rubber boots, or if you have L. L. Bean boots, the company will replace the rubber bottoms for you at a lot less than you'd pay for new models. Nevertheless, I wear cheap rubber boots and replace them when it's necessary.

I buy uninsulated rubber boots a size larger than my leather boots so that I can wear two pairs of heavy socks during cold weather. I also have sheepskin insoles, which help with warmth when cold weather arrives. I find insulated rubber boots too heavy for my liking, and my feet sweat badly in them. As long as I'm moving, uninsulated rubber boots worn with heavy socks and insoles—or lightly insulated leather boots, if there's no snow or if it's powdery—work best for me.

When you purchase boots for pheasant hunting, avoid the traditional Vibram soles. Footwear so equipped offers better traction, but that's usually not what you need in ringneck country. When it's muddy, those soles get clogged, thereby adding a bunch of weight to your feet. Vibram makes another

A hunter dressed properly for cold weather. He can raise his earflaps and unzip his collar if he gets too warm.

sole called Gumlite that works well, as do chain-style treads.

I've never taken to bib overalls, even those made especially for hunting and that are almost impossible to destroy. My preference runs to faced hunting pants. Most of the places in which I hunt pheasants don't have a lot of sharp things that poke and stab, although the facing comes in handy if I encounter something like multiflora rose. I also have a pair of heavy chaps, which I'll wear if it's extremely wet, if I need something to block a frigid wind, or if I want an extra layer of insulation from snow.

Most of the time when I'm hunting pheasants, I wear a shirt under a hunting vest rather than a hunting coat. The shirts run from lightweight cotton early in the season to heavier chamois cloth or wool later on.

233

I am probably a bad example of how to dress for cold-weather hunting. There have been entire seasons when I've haven't worn more than a cotton T-shirt, heavy hunting shirt, hooded sweatshirt, and vest on my upper body. That keeps me warm down close to zero, depending of course on the wind. But each person has to adjust to his own individual thermostat and dress accordingly.

I prefer a vest to a coat because I don't need the extra warmth and a vest allows me greater freedom of arm movement. If you do a lot of bird hunting, a good vest (or coat, if that is your preference) is worth the initial investment.

I have several requirements for a pheasant-hunting vest. First, and quite important to me, it has to be at least partly blaze orange. I always wear blaze orange no matter what a state's regulations may be. Next, a pheasant vest has to have a game pouch big enough to hold three roosters. Kansas hunters might say four birds, given the state's generous limit, but I'm not sure anyone makes a pouch that big.

I think that eight or ten shell loops are sufficient. You shouldn't have to shoot a half-box of shells to get a limit of ringnecks, but you may need extra ammo if you're in mixed-game country. If a vest has shell loops, they should be protected by pocket flaps. Exposed loops do not belong on a vest or coat that will be worn in briars and weeds. Before long, you'll have shredded loops and you'll start to lose shells. In fact, I have no problem with a vest that doesn't have loops, if it has roomy front pockets with flaps.

I have several vests, but just two of them see action come pheasant season. The first is a strap vest, brown with blaze orange accents, for warm-weather hunts. The second is a more conventional vest, solid blaze orange with a mesh back. Although my back is prone to sweating, I'll take a vest with a full-fabric back over a strap or mesh model with a vinyl-backed game pouch. Vinyl does a good job of keeping birds from bleeding through onto your shirt or pants, but it gives my back a bad case of the sweats.

The more traditional of my two vests sports quite a few "bells and whistles"—shell loops in the pockets, an interior (zippered) pocket for hunting license and other small "stuff," a special pocket for an electronic collar transmitter, and a zippered, drop-down game bag. I modified this vest by removing the Velcro tabs that close the front-pocket flaps. If pockets are deep enough, unless you take a serious tumble the flaps will keep the contents from falling out and debris from getting in.

If you're a "bare bones" kind of person and like a full vest, L. L. Bean makes its basic Upland Field Vest with buttons on the front and on the flap pockets (over shell loops), a roomy game bag, and that's it. But it only costs about forty dollars, and if you've priced serviceable hunting vests lately you know there aren't many out there for that kind of money. I wore an Upland Field Vest for years, still have it as a spare, and could still get by with it in a pinch.

Caps and gloves are two accessories to which many pheasant hunters give little thought. That's unfortunate, because in cold weather they are absolutely critical. Along with your feet, your hands and your head are the body parts most difficult to keep warm. If you do begin to overheat, uncovering your head and hands temporarily will help keep your internal thermostat at the proper setting.

I wear a variety of caps depending upon the weather. The

opener usually finds me in a mesh baseball cap that I exchange for one of solid cotton as the temperatures drop. If it's really frigid, I may wear a heavy stocking cap. All of my caps are blaze orange. The hooded sweatshirt that I wear in cold weather gives me the option of slipping the hood up over my cap, thus eliminating the need for extremely warm headgear.

Most hunters today wear baseball-style caps, which are quite practical. You should, however, avoid pulling the brim down too far if you're walking into the sun. A long brim can interfere with your shooting if you have the cap tugged down to shade your eyes; it will cause you to lift your head off the stock to see the bird. Expert shooters will also tell you that the underside of the brim should be dark (dark green is a good color) to avoid the reflection you might get from a lighter color, like blaze orange.

I don't care much for gloves, especially on my trigger hand. I prefer being able to feel the trigger and to operate the safety without a heavy layer between my skin and the metal. I've tried various kinds of light gloves for early-season shooting, and I've come full circle back to the baseball batting gloves I wore years ago. These gloves are rugged and tight fitting. Because I shoot traditional side-by-side shotguns where my left hand curls around the barrels, they also protect the bluing from excess wear. Until it gets below forty degrees, I usually don't wear a glove on my trigger hand. Some people favor light-leather shooting gloves, but I have small hands and have trouble finding ones that fit well. Batting gloves are easier to find in a variety of sizes, and the Velcro closure gives me a snug fit.

Some hunters like "trigger-finger mittens" for extreme

conditions. I bought a pair once, but found them too bulky and gave them to a friend who has trouble keeping his hands warm. I have a couple of pairs of leather gloves with a light, Thinsulate lining that keep my hands comfortable while allowing me good feel of the safety and triggers. Because my preferred pheasant gun has double triggers, I'm also some-what limited in how thick a glove I can wear and still have space for my finger inside the trigger guard.

One other valuable item of clothing is a pair of gaiters, like those worn by cross-country skiers. When hunting in deep, fluffy snow without gaiters, you have just two options—both of them bad. If you tuck your pants into your boots, moisture will eventually work inside onto your socks and down to your feet. If you leave pants outside of your boots, snow will get under them and chill your legs. Lightweight, waterproof gaiters will keep snow out of your boots and off your legs. Hunting in deep snow is uncomfortable enough without wor-rying about wet feet or cold legs.

Maps for Pheasant Hunters

Although much has been written about the value of maps for deer and turkey hunters, and for locating grouse and woodcock coverts, no one talks about map use by pheasant hunters. A good map will help you locate public hunting areas, get you back to that nice piece of private ground where you got permission last season, and provide the basis for pin-pointing new covers.

In my opinion, a pheasant hunter should have, at mini-mum, a series of maps covering the entire state in which he plans to hunt. I have two such series for Iowa. One is the *Iowa*

Atlas & Gazetteer, published by DeLorme Mapping. These are topographic maps, but they also give road names to help you keep track of your location. The other is the *Iowa Sportsman's Atlas*, which has a one-page map of every county. The DeLorme series covers just about all states, and I believe Midwestern states other than Iowa are included in the Sportsman's Atlas series.

Some state wildlife agencies provide excellent maps at little or no charge. South Dakota, for example, puts out a hunting atlas that shows all public hunting and Walk-In areas.

As I've mentioned elsewhere, if you do a lot of hunting in one or two counties, I'd suggest that you get a county plat book. These land-ownership references are usually available at county courthouses. They show property lines, provide names of owners and tenants of each piece of county land, and have alphabetical indexes that will give you landowner phone numbers.

Land ownership used to be pretty predictable, with the typical farmer living on and farming the same piece of ground. These days, however, a farmer may own a small piece of ground where he lives, but not farm anything within miles of his house. Or he may have additional farms, at some distance from his home place, that he owns, rents, or leases.

A plat book will give you an accurate idea of what the farmer is talking about when he says, "I've got another quarter-section you can hunt—a couple of miles north, then a mile west, then a half-mile north." I'm always a bit leery of getting complex directions straight, at which point I will whip out my plat book.

Be aware that ownership and lease agreements change fairly frequently. Always check with the farmer to be sure that eighty acres with the creek running through it three miles down the road is still his. It's a good idea to get a new plat book every three or four years in order to keep up with changes in boundaries and land ownership.

Spare Items and Other Necessary Gear

No, this section will not deal with extra tires for your vehicle, although that is one spare you shouldn't ignore on a hunting trip. What I am going to discuss here are items of gear related to a pheasant hunter's specific needs.

When I first started carrying spares, everything that I thought I might need fit into a gym bag. All I carried were extra shells, a change of socks, and a heavier or lighter shirt.

These days, I don't venture out without a fairly substantial duffel bag just about stuffed full. In the back of my pickup, I also have a couple of removable plastic drawers that fit under the wooden platform that supports my travel kennels. And my old gym bag with a complete, emergency change of clothes stays in the truck at all times.

My hunting duffel will usually have extra T-shirts and socks, a selection of gloves and caps for all conditions, a shirt appropriate for the weather, and a vest. I also have an old hunting coat that I leave in the truck all season. I don't wear it often, but it comes in handy if the weather turns nasty and I decide to keep hunting. There are spare boots in my emergency bag—older ones that will do in a pinch—but I'll often carry another pair in my big duffel.

Extra ammunition is especially important for oddballs like me who hunt with an uncommon gauge. Ever try to find 16-

gauge shells at the local convenience store? Or borrow them from your partners, all of whom shoot 12- and 20-gauge guns? In addition to the shells I have in my vest, I keep a spare box of 16-gauge ammo in one of the plastic drawers.

I always have a road map of the state in which I'm hunting, as well as the atlases and plat books I mentioned earlier. I keep mine in an old, zippered game bag—all that survives of a hunting coat from long ago. That bag also includes state hunting regulations, lists of public hunting areas, my notebook, and extra pens.

Along with what I've mentioned, my gear includes a pair of chaps, an idiot-proof camera for taking pictures in the field, and extra dog gear (bell, whistle, collar, and leash). I also carry two e-collars, which can be operated from the same transmitter, as well as spare batteries for both the transmitter and the collars.

Most serious pheasant hunters own at least one extra shotgun that fits them and with which they've done some shooting. You don't have to bring the spare on every hunt, but you may need it over the course of a long season.

Here I speak from experience. In 1980, my Sauer side-by-side took ill on a woodcock hunt and wasn't out of the "hospital" until after the end of pheasant season. I had an extra gun—nothing fancy, mind you, just a light and fast-handling Kasnar 20-gauge over-and-under with double triggers. I'd shot a couple of rounds of skeet with the gun when I first got it, then relegated it to the closet.

The Kasnar got its call on the opening day of the 1980 grouse season, which happened to be the best year for ruffed grouse I've ever seen in Iowa. I had fourteen shots—many of them easy—and as far as I could tell, I didn't touch a feather. Only cooler heads in my hunting party kept me from wrapping that over-and-under around a tree.

I finally discovered that the gun simply did not fit. On the skeet range I could hit clays with the gun shouldered, but when I brought it up on flushing grouse or pheasants, the fit wasn't even close.

The next time that the Sauer 16 gauge failed me was in November 1985, right in the middle of pheasant season. This time I switched to an old Ithaca 16-gauge side-by-side with which I had taken the time to become familiar. I shot about 50 percent with that gun for the rest of the season. Not great, but far better than I'd done with my previous spare. Although the stock fit on my two 16-gauge guns wasn't a perfect match, they were both double-trigger side-by-sides. It also helped that I had used the Ithaca on grouse and woodcock, some preserve birds, and at skeet.

Part of the beauty of buying a spare gun is that you can justify spending extra bucks and off-season hours prowling sporting-goods shops and gun shows. Your spare gun be similar to what you're accustomed to, or you should take the time to become adequately acquainted with it. For instance, if you're a pump gunner I wouldn't suggest an autoloader as a backup. You may find yourself trying to pump a fixed forend.

You don't need to break the family budget on a spare gun. Better to spend more money on a really good primary gun, which won't break down often anyhow. As long as your backup gun works and you can shoot it, it doesn't have to be anything fancy. If your main shotgun is one you'd rather protect when conditions are nasty, you can look at your spare as a

A well-prepared hunter should carry a variety of spares, including an extra dog and gun, when he takes off to hunt for several days.

"rainy day gun." Also, shooting a backup when you want to protect your better gun will get you sufficiently familiar with it if it must temporarily become your everyday gun.

The Benefits of More Than One Dog

Serious pheasant hunters should consider owning a second dog. I've found that hunting dogs are far more prone to breakdown than are shotguns. And unlike a gun, their life expectancy can be extended just so far even given the best of care.

Hunters who don't get out that often during the season probably cannot justify owning two dogs in their prime. Limited time afield doesn't provide enough work to keep more than one canine in top form. However, if you have only one dog, another of Brown's Laws of Pheasant Hunting states that your four-footed partner is almost certain to be afflicted with something during the course of the season, leaving you dogless for a period of time.

During the last twenty-two seasons, I've hunted over seven of my own pheasant dogs. And I've lost at least a part of a season with every dog I've owned. They've had abscesses, worms, and broken bones, along with more serious problems such as kidney failure and cancer. Rebel hunted for four years with bad kidneys and was not an all-day dog, particularly in extremes of temperature. Jake had hip dysplasia, although he didn't hunt like it and it wasn't diagnosed until he was six. But it was Jake's lesser illnesses and injuries that made me realize I needed a minimum of two dogs at all times.

Since 1985, I've been down to one dog twice, and in both cases it was because of an unexpected loss. Jake died suddenly in December 1986, leaving Rebel as my only dog for the last month or so of that season. Although Rebel's kidneys had been questionable since she was three, she did well until the disease claimed her life in 1991. My Gordon setter Gwen was only a five-month-old pup at the time, but fortunately Heidi stayed healthy throughout the season. By the next year, Gwen was ready to pick up a share of the load.

Of the dogs I've owned over more than two decades, only Heidi lived to hunt beyond her tenth birthday. And in speaking with other serious hunters, I am convinced that any time a hunting dog is still active in its double-digit years, you should count yourself lucky. Ten is old for any dog, but gun dogs are rather like cars and trucks—it isn't the years that matter, it's the mileage.

As I said, casual hunters usually can't justify owning more than one adult dog. But sportsmen in that category may want to consider acquiring a pup about the time their mature hunter hits five to seven years old. If you wait too long, an older dog may have trouble adjusting to a rambunctious youngster in its life. If things work out as they should, your pup will come along gradually while your old-timer carries the brunt of the hunting duties. And when the old dog is ready for retirement, the youngster will be groomed for his slot in the starting lineup and you won't have to go through a season with a pup that's still too young for "prime time" duty.

If you do get caught dogless or find yourself with an oldster that's slowed considerably and is able to hunt only for brief periods, there are possibilities other than pups. As I discussed in Chapter Five, you can purchase either a finished dog or a started dog. Although even a started dog will cost substantially more than a pup, the price can be a bargain if you tally how much you'd spend on food, vet bills, training birds, and maybe professional training in a dog's first year of life.

Even if you have two adult dogs, this does not mean you have to hunt them together. If I'm going out for only a half-day hunt, I'll usually leave one of my dogs at home. But on a typical, all-day hunt, my tactic is to work one dog for a couple of hours, change animals, then finish the day with the first dog. This gives you an animal that is well rested at all times. I believe that it is easier on dogs in the long run—which translates to better performance—if you do not hunt one dog every day for most of a two- or three-month season.

Another advantage of having two dogs, assuming they are of different breeds or different hunting styles, is that you can pick the dog that fits the situation. Heidi and Rebel were my team for four seasons, and they had very different styles. Heidi was excellent along narrow waterways, ditches, and fence-rows, while Rebel was in her element in big CRP fields.

Depending on how hard you hunt, you may decide that owning two dogs is more of a necessity than a luxury. For me, it is well worth the time and expense to maintain a second dog for the advantage it gives me during the brief months of the hunting season.

Ethics in Pheasant Hunting

I have heard ethics defined as the way you behave when you're by yourself and you're sure no one will see you. Ethics in hunting are especially important because much of the time there is, in fact, no one around to referee your behavior. Even if you stay within the letter of the law, do you occasionally do things you wouldn't tell your buddies about? Maybe temptation got the best of you and you ground-swatted a healthy rooster. Although that isn't illegal in most places, it is the kind of behavior that hunters would consider unethical, or at least frown upon.

Ethics vary, often widely, from person to person. When selecting hunting partners, finding someone whose ethics are compatible with yours is important. For example, a lot of pheasant hunters practice "party shooting." In other words, if there are three of you hunting and the daily limit is three roosters, you have a party limit of nine birds. It makes no difference whether you each shoot three or whether one person shoots five, another three, and the bad shot of the group only one. You still get your party limit.

Strictly speaking, shooting party limits is illegal in most places. However, it is not something with which you are likely to be charged by a game warden, unless you are foolish enough to put five roosters in your game vest. If you throw three limits of birds in the back of a pickup, who is to know which hunter shot how many?

The point is that you know, and if you are uncomfortable about it, you should make your feelings clear to the other members of your group. If I'm hunting with strangers, I let them know that I prefer to shoot my own birds, and that I'm not interested in shooting theirs. I have engaged in party shooting on a few occasions, and I didn't feel right about it.

Of course there are gray areas that even the most stringent code of ethics cannot cover. I rarely hunt without one of my own dogs, and they are often doing the bird finding for other hunters. If I shoot my limit but the others are short of theirs, what do I do? Whistle up my dogs and say, "Sorry guys, but that's it"?

I've had that situation happen often enough that I've arrived at a solution that fits my personal code of conduct. I stay in the field as long as the rest of the party wishes to do so, but I shoot only to finish a crippled bird that might otherwise escape. In my ethical code it is more important to recover a crippled rooster than to worry if I actually kill one too many birds.

Ethics are not absolute, and you should not think that everyone will agree with your definitions. My ethics are significantly different from my father's. He shot far more pheasants on the ground than he ever did in the air. I accepted that in him, both because he taught me so many valuable things about hunting, and because he was the product of a different era. I would not accept the same behavior from my hunting contemporaries.

The Hunter's Notebook

Hunters have been keeping records of their exploits afield for well over a century. In my own case, I have to give George Bird Evans credit for inspiring me to do so. I read his book *The Upland Shooting Life* while I was overseas. When I returned to Iowa in 1973, I started recording my hunts.

Like Evans, I've discovered that my notes have grown more detailed over the years. I started using three-by-five-inch pocket notebooks, and would often get two or three entries on a page. I've since graduated to a larger variety, and I will commonly fill a page with one day's hunt.

After listing the date, I enter a synopsis of the day's hunt. I record the location, number of birds moved, points by my dogs, how many shots I took, and how many birds I hit. I also mention how I hunted the cover and how the birds reacted. I may add a note to myself concerning a better way to tackle the particular spot the next time I hunt it. Then I conclude with the time of day and the weather—temperature, wind direction and velocity, cloud cover, and ground conditions.

Rereading these notes can be an educational experience. You will be able to evaluate your own shooting and your dog's work over multiple seasons. You may also pick up patterns of behavior by the birds under given conditions. But even if you don't learn anything—though you almost certainly will—notebooks are an excellent way of jogging your memory about past hunts. I can go back to my first diary, now nearly thirty years old, and remember those long-gone moments with my Moroccan-born Brittany Deke, and the frustrations of trying to get him to adapt to Iowa pheasants.

My notes are by no means works of literature. They are the jottings of a tired hunter, usually written as I take a break after one field and before I tackle the next, or after the hunt is over. Although they form the basis of this book, in notebook form they are of value to no one but me. Yet to me they are price-less because they contain memories of dogs and men who hunt no more, of places where the cover and the birds disap-peared a decade ago, and of good times alone or with boon companions. They are the best way I know to relive seasons past. And in the too-long interval that stretches from the end of one season to the beginning of the next, they help make the time pass quicker.

TEN

Pheasants Forever

In this final chapter, I'm going to look at the future of pheasant hunting. Not coincidentally, the chapter's title is also the name of a national organization, Pheasants Forever, whose goal is to improve pheasant populations through habitat protection and restoration. I'll examine Pheasants Forever and what it has accomplished in the two decades since it was founded.

If we expect to make any kind of accurate prediction about the future of pheasant populations, we have to look at the past. If we can determine when and why the birds prospered and when and why they declined, we can then make an educated guess as to what the future holds.

First, bear with me for a moment while I review certain critical events in pheasant-habitat management history that I have presented elsewhere in this book.

A Review of Pheasant Ups and Downs
The reasons for highs and lows in pheasant populations vary from region to region. However, the major factor in maintaining healthy bird populations anywhere is the availability of

proper habitat. Although significant changes in bird numbers from one year to the next may occur because of extreme weather factors—severe winters or cold, wet nesting seasons—over the long term the birds will recover if they have the right habitat.

In the Midwest, pheasant numbers tended to remain high during periods of agricultural diversity. Most veteran Iowa hunters can remember when the average farm was about two hundred to three hundred acres in size. The typical farmer had some livestock and a number of small fields planted in different crops. You were likely to find oats, alfalfa, corn, and soybeans all on the same small farm, with no single field larger than forty acres.

That situation changed gradually. Livestock operations have grown much larger and farmers now tend to specialize in either cattle or hogs. Many landowners have no livestock at all and plant their acreage in row crops.

The Soil Bank, a popular set-aside program, ended in the early 1960s. That loss along with existing changes in agricultural practices eliminated much of the remaining nesting and winter cover. Farmers had already removed numerous fencerows and planted row crops in their place. When the Soil Bank Program ended, pheasants lost large blocks of cover where they had reproduced and found refuge from the weather for years.

Because the changes were gradual, along with the fact that pheasants are hardy and adaptable birds, there were no immediate, drastic declines in bird numbers. But following hard winters or poor nesting seasons, numbers tumbled. Unlike the past, when plenty of good habitat was available, the birds no longer recovered even when nesting and weather conditions were favorable.

In some states, the bottom dropped out. Formerly good pheasant-hunting states, such as Michigan and Ohio, saw their harvest plummet to lows they could not have anticipated. In Minnesota, the yearly harvest went from close to a million birds in the early 1960s to one-third of that by 1980.

Even in top pheasant states, numbers fell drastically. In 1984, Iowa experienced a record-low harvest of seven hundred thousand birds. In 1986, South Dakota biologists estimated their state's total pheasant population at 1.8 million birds—a fifteen-year low. The region was paying the price for habitat changes that had occurred over the previous twenty years.

But by 1987, Iowa's pheasant harvest had doubled. In recent years, South Dakota bird numbers have hit a thirty-year high. What made the difference?

The long-term answer is habitat, due in large part to the Conservation Reserve Program established under the 1985 Farm Bill. By 1987, the additional CRP-based nesting and winter cover had a significant impact in both Iowa and South Dakota. When CRP enrollment peaked in 1991, the two states between them had over four million acres enrolled in the program.

There were still ups and downs due to capricious Midwestern winters, but for the most part bird numbers remained strong through the 1990s. South Dakota experienced some severe winters during the 1990s and did have temporary drops in bird numbers. But with 1.4 million acres enrolled in the CRP as of 2000, the birds had excellent habitat and bounced back after each dip.

However, the reauthorized 1996 Farm Bill brought significant changes to Iowa. The loss of half of its CRP ground was especially critical in the state's northern tier, which had little quality habitat left once the CRP acres reverted to crop ground. When the state suffered one of its longest and snowiest winters in 2000, followed by a wet, cold nesting season in the spring of 2001, the result was the worst pheasant harvest in Iowa history. Less than a half-million roosters were taken during the 2001 season, a harvest close to a quarter-million birds below the previous all-time low.

CRP was retained (in fact, the program was expanded slightly) under the 2002 Farm Bill. Although it's unlikely that Iowa will again see the peak CRP enrollments of the early 1990s, there is reason to be optimistic about a rebound in bird numbers.

As Farming Goes, So Goes the Pheasant

With the possible exception of the bobwhite quail, no other popular gamebird is as closely tied to agriculture as the pheasant. The ringneck's fate hinges directly upon whatever direction farming takes.

The days when a farmer planted crops and raised livestock solely for economic survival and the preservation of his land are gone forever. It is not uncommon for a modern farmer to make more money from government subsidies than he does from selling what he produces. Washington keeps commodity prices artificially low to protect consumers. At the same time, our government encourages the highest possible crop yields by basing its subsidy payments on what the farmer has produced over a given period of time.

In turn, this results in the utilization of all available

modern technology, including herbicides and pesticides.

But the public is expressing legitimate concerns about water and air quality. The government is attempting to respond to these concerns and to worries that overly intensive crop production is causing excessive erosion of irreplaceable topsoil.

The result is a national "farm policy" that seems to make little sense to anyone. The federal government warns about the hazards of smoking, yet subsidizes the production of tobacco. It indirectly encourages overproduction of commodities such as corn, then pays farmers to take land out of production in order to avoid surpluses.

Although the overall policy seldom seems to make much sense, elements of it do—one such element is the CRP. As I have emphasized previously, pheasants—and pheasant hunters—end up being big winners in this program. The dramatic upsurge in bird numbers in the Midwest is directly attributable to the CRP. Take away the program and pheasant populations could easily return to where they were in the early 1980s.

Fortunately, because the CRP provision of the farm policy works well both for farmers and for Washington, it is hard to envision its demise. But there will be modifications. Under the 1996 Farm Bill, for example, additional emphasis was placed on water-quality management through the Buffer Strip Initiative of the CRP. (Buffers strips are parcels of cover ninety-nine feet wide and adjacent to waterways.) Landowners are paid a bonus for establishing and maintaining buffer strips because of their importance in controlling water quality and soil erosion.

Although Iowa lost many of its larger blocks of CRP land when the program's emphasis changed, the Buffer Strip Initiative has been extremely popular. The state now leads the nation in buffer-strip acres enrolled. In an excellent example of cooperation between two levels of government and a private conservation organization, the U.S. Department of Agriculture's Natural Resources Conservation Service (NRCS), the Iowa Department of Natural Resources, and Pheasants Forever have combined their efforts as a driving force behind this program. The result is a reestablishment of critical CRP wildlife habitat in parts of the state where it is badly needed.

It takes a program of this scale, with millions of acres taken out of crop production and replaced by suitable habitat, to impact bird numbers in a big way. Most pheasants live their lives on or near farms. What happens to the cover on those farms determines what happens to the birds.

Given the amount of money involved in the CRP set-aside initiatives, it is impossible for individual states or private groups, even working together, to have a major impact on patterns of land use. When you understand that many Iowa farmers are paid over $100 per acre annually for their CRP ground (over $150 for buffer strips) and that about 1.8 million acres of Iowa farmland is enrolled, you begin to see the economic scope of the program. Good agricultural ground is too expensive to buy or lease on a large scale for anyone but Uncle Sam to operate a program the size of the CRP.

However, states can "sweeten the pot" to encourage landowners to not only provide wildlife habitat, but also make their land available to hunters. Under its popular Walk-In Areas program, South Dakota's Department of Game, Fish and

Parks leases nearly one million acres of private land for hunting. Under this program, the state guarantees the landowner a monetary return and removes the hassle of dealing directly with hunters. Kansas and Nebraska have similar, but smaller-scale programs.

Although the conservation provisions of the 2002 Farm Bill look positive for wildlife, the old saying about the devil being in the details applies here. One potentially significant problem with the 2002 bill is that it authorizes new programs while it retains the old ones. Some state biologists feel that the NRCS isn't adequately staffed to reach out to all private landowners and explain the benefits of the new programs to them. And the way the federal government works, if the funds in a program aren't utilized, the money isn't reauthorized.

Also, as in any government program, there are certain inequities. One of my farmer friends wanted to put an entire three-hundred-fifty-acre farm into the CRP shortly after the program was first authorized. His farm, however, was initially rejected by the NRCS. It was not erodible, they told him, because of all the terraces he had built. Meanwhile farms around him—on which the owners had done little or nothing to prevent erosion—were being accepted into the CRP. Although my friend's farm was accepted into the program a couple of years later, it is easy to understand why many farmers believe that Washington gives the biggest rewards to the least conservation-minded landowners.

That is why we should thank farmers who work their land with conservation in mind. Whether they do it because of a federal program, Pheasants Forever, or to enhance wildlife habitat, it's of benefit to everyone.

Fee Hunting for Pheasants

Most of hunters past the age of fifty remember when fee hunting for wild pheasants was unheard of—the privilege was free for the asking. But as we head deeper into the twenty-first century, some pheasant hunters wonder whether free hunting will be gradually replaced by fee hunting.

In the U.S., the first type of fee hunting to gain widespread acceptance was the shooting preserve. With these operations, hunting was considered a business: The preserve owner provided goods—in most cases feathered game—for clients who were willing to pay for them.

Once the province of the wealthy, shooting preserves now have a much broader client base. In fact, the preserve business is booming in many parts of the country. Where game is scarce or land access is limited, this popularity is easy to understand. But why are preserves doing so well in parts of the country, such as the Midwest, where pheasant hunting is still good and where it is not difficult to find a place to hunt?

There are several answers to this question. One is that in most states preserves are able to offer a long open season. In Iowa, which has a generous two-and-a-half-month pheasant season, the preserve season is open from September through March.

Convenience is another reason for the popularity of preserves. Older hunters, for example, may still have the physical capacity to shoot birds, but not to walk the long distances often required by wild-bird hunting. Likewise, at the other end of the age spectrum, fathers introducing sons to hunting may wish to do so in a setting where they know game will be found and youthful interest will remain high.

These days, a growing number of pheasant hunters own dogs. Preserves provide excellent opportunities for sportsmen to train and polish their canine companions. Preserve birds can be used for preseason, gun-dog tune-ups or midseason hunts when wild-bird numbers are down. Shooting preserves are perfect for "senior" dogs too old to hunt wild birds.

And finally, the cost is well within what the market will bear. Typically, preserve pheasants start at under $20 for each bird released, which isn't bad when you consider the time, effort, and mileage involved in bagging a limit of wild ring-necks.

In addition to the idea of paying for pheasants, the concern expressed by most hunters who have not experienced preserve shooting is how much of a challenge the "tame" birds offer. Although I don't hunt preserves a lot, I have sampled several and can assure you that for the average hunter it's not like the proverbial shooting of fish in a barrel. All in all, while I find them easier than wild birds, pen-raised pheasants pose enough challenge to maintain most hunters' interest.

If preserve pheasants are properly raised, handled, and released, they often display the same bag of tricks used by their wild relatives. Although preserve birds are not well equipped to evade their natural enemies, they can do a pretty good job of eluding two-legged predators.

Having said that, I admit that I don't really enjoy hunting preserve pheasants. While I don't want to pay to shoot sitting "ducks," I would at least like a chance at some return on the bucks I shell out for released birds. Too often, pen-raised pheasants either run off or flush wild.

That doesn't mean that I don't visit preserves. Typically, I

Donner, the author's German shorthair, retrieves a chukar on a preserve hunt. Preserve hunting can be enjoyable and helpful in dog training, though the author prefers to shoot either chukar or quail rather than released pheasants.

hunt a preserve at least once each year, though I usually shoot quail or chukar rather than pheasants. My dogs benefit more from these birds because they are less likely than pheasants to depart the area before we have a chance at them.

Given the growth in popularity of locking up land in sporting leases, some people see that type of fee hunting as the wave of the future. I'm not sure that view is valid.

In Iowa, there has been a significant increase in the amount of land leased for deer and turkey hunting. Waterfowl leases are common in many states, and quail leases tend to be the rule on Texas ranches. With waterfowl, you've got migrating birds to restock your lease. Texas quail leases run to thousands of acres, with the cost usually split between several hunters.

But there are differences where pheasant hunting is con-cerned. Throughout much of prime pheasant range, farms and ranches are more modest in size. While pheasants may move into good cover once the shooting starts, that can't provide the level of "restocking" necessary to maintain high numbers.

If the landowner is smart, he isn't going to lease for less money than he needs to cover expenses. In some states, a farmer's general liability coverage has been ruled to be suffi-cient if he grants permission to hunt without charging. However, if he's leasing or charging a trespass fee, the state then sees his land use as recreational as well as agricultural, which means he needs costly, additional liability coverage.

At the going rate for pheasant leases—keep in mind they increase annually—most landowners aren't going to get rich. In 2000, the South Dakota Department of Game, Fish and Parks was paying about $1.50 an acre to lease private ground and open it to public hunting. As of 2002, $5 an acre is the highest, private-lease rate I have heard of where only pheasants are involved. By way of example, if you pay $5 an acre to lease a section, or six hundred and forty acres, you're laying out $3,200. If you take one hundred ringnecks off that section—a good bag, even from high-quality habitat—you're paying $32 a bird. That's steep in comparison to other options.

As I've mentioned, in South Dakota it's common for landowners to charge a daily trespass fee per gun. If you can hunt for $50 a day, you're ahead of the lease-agreement exam-ple I just described even if you shoot just two roosters. It pays to do the math ahead of time.

There is a variety of guide and outfitting services available to pheasant hunters. They range from small operations that provide only the land, a guide, and a dog to large outfitters that furnish everything—license, dogs, food, lodging, bird cleaning and packaging, and ground transportation. Costs vary in proportion to the services offered and run the gamut from cut-rate to premium fees of hundreds of dollars per hunter per day. As always, it's a question of what the market will bear and the type of experience sportsmen desire.

Fee hunting is a reality that will continue to expand. Whether the costs are for a small-time guide or a big-time outfitter, a land-lease arrangement or a daily trespass charge, there will always be a market. Essentially, you are paying someone to take some of the risk out of your pheasant-hunting trip. You may be paying for a place to hunt, for someone to help you find birds, or both. In theory and often in fact, the more you pay, the more you reduce the risk of striking out. Of course there are few guarantees in pheasant hunting. A high-cost shoot may end up as a bust, while bargain-basement hunt may prove to be a real find. How happy you are with what you get from fee hunting depends on your discretionary income, your expectations, and what it takes to satisfy you.

Pheasants Forever

That brings us this dynamic organization of people—most of them hunters—concerned about pheasants, and the story of what they have accomplished in the two decades since the group was founded.

Pheasants Forever (PF) got its start partially through the efforts of an outdoor journalist who wrote an article in 1981 addressing the plight of the pheasant in Minnesota. The writer suggested creating an organization to aid the plummeting pheasant population, much as Ducks Unlimited had responded to the waterfowl crisis of the 1930s. The idea received overwhelming response, and PF was born.

The first PF chapter was formed in 1983 and had an almost immediate impact in Minnesota. That same year the state passed legislation requiring a $5 pheasant-hunting stamp. In its first year, the stamp program generated a half-million dollars to aid pheasant restoration.

By 2002, PF had grown to five hundred and fifty chapters and ninety thousand members nationally. Pheasant hunters have responded to the organization even in states with good bird numbers. Iowa, for example, has more pheasants than people. Yet in its ninety-nine counties, there are over one hundred PF chapters.

Superficially, PF resembles other wildlife and habitat conservation organizations; that is, the group raises most of its money through annual banquets. However, PF differs from other organizations in one important way: With the exception of membership dues, all money raised by the local chapters is retained by them for local projects. Pheasant Forever impacts habitat in its members' backyard.

Although PF focuses on local projects, it does not operate in a vacuum. The organization has pushed for the renewal and expansion of the CRP in the 1996 and 2002 Farm Bills, as well as the inclusion of other wildlife-friendly conservation initiatives. And PF regularly partners with state and federal agencies in implementing these programs on the ground. In Iowa, these partnerships have resulted in the establishment of over three hundred thousand CRP acres, most of those under the program's Buffer Strip Initiative.

In many areas, especially those prone to severe winters, a lack of trees can be a problem for pheasant survival. Shelterbelts, which protected birds from the impact of blizzards, have been removed. Since its inception, PF has worked to restore this valuable habitat by planting over eighty thousand acres of woody cover. Although there are state and federal programs available to landowners, by combining PF money and effort with government dollars, shelterbelt plantings become more attractive to farmers.

Food plots are also important, especially when they are planted in proximity to shelter in those areas where winter cover is in short supply. During the winter, pheasants have to eat more in order to maintain their body temperatures. Food plots positioned close to cover allow birds to eat with less exposure to predators. As of 2001, Pheasants Forever has planted close to eight hundred thousand acres of food plots.

When land is purchased by private conservation groups, it provides permanent cover not subject to the capriciousness of federal or state programs nor to changes in farming practices. Although land acquisition can be expensive, PF has purchased seventy-seven thousand acres of habitat for public hunting.

When I wrote the first edition of this book, Pheasants Forever—not yet a decade old—had a ten-year goal of restoring one million acres of habitat. Now, as the organization celebrates its twentieth anniversary, it has beneficially impacted almost two million acres of land in support of wildlife conservation. Before the creation of PF, no one could have imagined that a private organization could have such large-scale influence upon pheasant habitat. What Pheasants Forever brought to the "pheasant issue" was an awareness that the birds were

This proud youngster, with his first rooster taken over a fine dog, is part of the next generation of hunters.

in trouble, backed by a willingness to do something about it.

One ongoing danger is that pheasant hunters might look at big federal programs, such as the CRP, and think that their involvement in organizations like PF is no longer necessary. Fortunately, this has not happened—PF has continued to grow and combine its efforts with those of state and federal agencies to get "the most bang for the buck."

In summary, the future of the pheasant, at least in the heart of its range across the Midwest, looks better than anyone would have imagined back in the early 1980s. As I write this, we're coming off a season during which Iowa, Kansas, and Nebraska experienced near-record-low bird harvests. However, with the reauthorization and expansion of the CRP under the 2002 Farm Bill, the creation of additional smaller-

In this hunter education class, students had a chance to take what they learned into the field and shoot preserve pheasants.

scale programs, and the efforts of PF and landowners, the potential is there for the birds to recover.

The Next Generation of Pheasant Hunters

As we head into the twenty-first century, we must also think of the future of pheasant hunters. Hunting is under attack in many parts of the country. Young people today have many more recreational opportunities from which to choose than did those of us who started hunting twenty or more years ago. Without some effort on the part of today's hunters, there are likely to be far fewer of us in the future. The dual threat of an increase in anti-hunters and a decrease in new hunters does not bode well for our sport.

But putting legions of hunters into the field is not the

answer. We must teach the new generation, and we must do it better than we were taught. Illegal and unsportsmanlike practices that were commonplace and for the most part overlooked in the past cannot be tolerated now or in in the future. We no longer live in a world where people hunt or don't hunt, yet still respect each other's rights. We now face a situation where many of those who don't hunt are openly hostile to those of us who do.

Hunter education programs, now required of new hunters in most states, offer a unique opportunity to start the next generation off right. Not long ago, hunting was a tradition handed down from father to son. That's the way I learned, as did most hunters of my generation. Today, with fewer hunters—and with more children being raised by a single parent, usually the mother—this is less true. But many women are showing an interest in hunting. I get a good feeling when a mother with her son or daughter attends one of our hunter education courses.

A program called Becoming an Outdoors Woman is growing and drawing women into the traditionally male world of hunting. All too often, we've excluded wives, sisters, and daughters from hunting. Becoming an Outdoors Woman gives them an opportunity to learn about hunting (and other outdoor activities) in a setting other than all-male.

There is a groundswell of environmental activism in this country, and we must make sure that hunters are a part of it. When we champion sound conservation practices, even the nonhunting environmentalists begin to see us as part of the solution rather than part of the problem. We must establish common cause with all environmentally concerned groups, not just with other hunters. In so doing, we can isolate and thwart the efforts of radical anti-hunters.

Hunters have a proud heritage of always being at the forefront of conservation movements, and we shouldn't be afraid to remind everyone of this fact. For generations we've been paying for wildlife habitat through our license dollars, memberships in conservation groups, and self-imposed excise taxes on firearms and ammunition. Others are only now awakening to the fact that there is a cost to protecting the environment, and that we cannot rely solely on state and federal tax revenues to pay the bill. Those of us who derive enjoyment from nature and wildlife should be willing to open our wallets and express our commitment in tangible form.

From the vantage point of the present, the future looks bright. The pheasant hunters of the twenty-first century have challenges to face, mostly as a result of a rapidly changing world and of shifting societal values. But with dedication and the support of organizations like Pheasants Forever, they can make that group's name more than just a title.

May there be pheasants forever, as long as there are hunters who are worthy of them.